This book is dedicated to the memory of Robert Cargni-Mitchell.

Special Thanks

Nick Bowler, Maud Burnett McInerney, Sarah Hicks, Melissa Pardo-Bunte and Kristina Vos-Petersen

Also by Benjamin McVoy

References in the Books of Monty Python Vol. One: Big Red Book and Brand New Bok or Papperbok

Preface

I probably started watching *Fawlty Towers* around age ten. That would have been two years after series two first aired in the U. K. I found it very funny and understood almost all of the jokes. However, there were some things, like cricket, that I knew very little about at that time. *Fawlty Towers* is one of those shows so densely packed with humor that I felt that the episodes were worth dissecting to understand them entirely.

In this volume I have supplied explanations for the references not only in the show itself, but also in the DVD commentary provided by John Cleese. I am aware that there are some reference guides already online, but mine is more comprehensive. I include items that I have not seen included in any guide. For example, I identified the Chopin composition that is played on the tape deck in the episode *The Wedding Party*.

Now that you know a little more about my perspective, I hope that this book can provide both enlightenment and pleasure.

Contents

Episode One – A Touch of Class

Bars – "I had two bars." In this instance Basil is referring to musical bars, which are measurements of length in a composition. He is saying that he only had the time to listen to two bars of Brahms' Third Symphony.

Beaujolais – The name of a wine from the Province of Beaujolais in France. The history of the wine can be traced back to the Roman Empire. Most of the Beaujolais wines are made with Gamay grapes. The grape has a thin skin and is low in tannins. The wine itself is generally light-bodied and contains a high acid content.

Brahms' Third Racket – Johannes Brahms (1833 – 1897) was a German composer born in Hamburg during the mid-Romantic period. His Symphony No. 3 in F major, Op. 90 is what Basil calls Brahms' Third Racket.

British Empire coins – Coins that are from Great Britain and territories claimed by Great Britain during the time of the empire.

Cash a check – In today's world the act of cashing a check is probably rarer and rarer. In the case of Lord Melbury, he most likely wrote a check out to Basil Fawlty in exchange for bank notes.

C. I. D. - The Criminal Investigation Department is a branch of the police in United Kingdom police departments. The officers are plainclothes detectives.

The first C. I. D. was a branch of the Metropolitan Police and was formed in 1878.

Copes Copy Coupon – This is probably a betting form for a football pool. It is a form that Basil is filling out at the front desk. It is only visible for a couple of frames. It seems to have nothing to do with the episode so probably the props department provided it randomly. However, it is possible that this is a sort of Easter egg. After all, according to the events in *Communication Problems,* Basil does like to bet.

Country Life – A British magazine founded in 1897. It is devoted to aspects of rural UK life. Each issue begins with several pages containing advertisements for upscale residential properties. Presumably, it was among those pages that Basil's ad for Fawlty Towers was included.

Crème Portugaise – Also known as Cream Soup Portuguese, it is a cream soup mixed with tomato puree made using sliced bacon and a dry-cooked rice garnish.

D'Oliveira, Basil - (Basil Lewis "Dolly" D'Oliveira; 1931 – 2011) D'Oliveira was an English international cricket player whose background was South African Cape Coloured. He played county cricket for Worcestershire. When England included him for a tour of South Africa it caused a controversy known as The Dolly Affair. The apartheid government objected to him on the basis of his mixed race.

Duke of Buckleigh – The title Duke of Buckleigh does not seem to exist.

Dustbins – A British term meaning "garbage can."

Dustmen – A British term meaning "garbage collectors."

Gin and orange – An alcoholic drink containing gin and orange juice and often an orange wedge.

Half bottle – A half bottle of wine holds 375 milliliters (about 12.68 oz).

Hundred – It is when a batsman gets 100 runs in one inning. Also known as a "century."

Lemon squash – A concentrated syrup used in beverage making. In this case, it may refer to a non-alcoholic beverage consisting of lemon squash and carbonated water. There are many variations of the drink, some alcoholic and some not.

Lloyd's Bank – During the scene in the town a sign can be seen for a branch of Lloyd's Bank. It is the largest commercial and retail bank in Great Britain.

Me old mucker- Mucker is idiomatic English meaning "friend." It is primarily used in the UK.

MI5 – Short for Military Intelligence, Section 5, it is the United Kingdom's domestic counter-intelligence and security agency.

Peer of the realm – A member of the class of peers that has the right to sit at the House of Lords.

Potato Famine - The Irish Potato Famine, known in Irish Gaelic as "an Drochshao," lasted from 1845 to 1852. The period was one of starvation and disease which led to social crisis and had a large impact on Irish history.

Rotter – According to Oxford Languages, a rotter is "a cruel, stingy or unkind person."

Scotch and water – A mixture of Scottish whisky and water. Some people believe that a few drops of water help to release the flavor of whisky.

Sir Richard and Lady Morris – There have been a few people named Sir Richard Morris. The author can find no reason to believe that the character in *Fawlty Towers* was named after any one of them.

Sotheby's - The world's largest broker of fine art and decorative objects. Although it was founded by Samuel Baker in London in 1744, its headquarters are in New York.

Toffee-nosed – A way to say "snobbish" that is primarily used in Great Britain.

Tone – The character of a place. As Basil says, "We're losing tone."

French:

> **Carte de vins** – Wine list

> **Bon appétit** - Enjoy your meal

> **Naturellement** - Naturally

> **Je ne sais quoi** – Idiomatic French meaning "I don't know what, but it has something special."

Spanish:

¿Qué? - What?

Señor - Mister

Uno, dos, tres – One, two, three

Mucho burro alli – *Basil is trying to say that there is "too much butter there." Instead, he says that there are* "lots of donkeys there."

Mantequilla - Butter

Por favor - Please

Si - Yes

Mantequilla, solamente, dos – Butter, only, two.

Arriba – *Saying "arriba" to someone is a way of giving the person encouragement or energizing the person.*

Entender - Understand

Obteuer la valise – *This is nonsensical Spanish from Basil asking Manuel to get the suitcase.*

La valise en el, er, auto bianco sportive – *This is nonsensical Spanish from Basil trying to explain to Manuel that the suitcase is in the white sports car.*

Y a la sala siete por favor – And to room seven please.

Pronto – Soon, promptly

Sirvase buscar mi equipaje que esta en el automovil blanco y lo traer a la sala numero siete. - Please look for my luggage in the white car and bring it to room number seven.

Señor habla español - Gentleman speaks Spanish.

Solo un poco. Lo siento. Pero he olvidado mucho – Just a little. I am sorry, but I have forgotten a lot.

No, no, habla muy bien. Muy muy bien. Formidable! - No, no, he speaks very well. Very, very well. Terrific!

Gracias, gracias – Thank you, thank you.

Lo voy a coger ahora – I'm going to take it now.

Si señor - Yes, sir.

¿Qué? - What?

No entender – I don't understand.

Prenda las casos en - *This is nonsensical Spanish from Basil.*

Ole – *An expression of excitement or joy.*

From the commentary by John Cleese

Accents

> **Cockney** – An English dialect and accent spoken primarily in the East End of London by the working-class and the lower middle-class.

> **Essex** – An English accent from the Essex area that features a lot of lapsed consonants.

Berkeley, Ballard - (Ballard Blascheck; 1904 – 1988) An English actor who played Major Gowan in both series of *Fawlty Towers*. He also had parts in *The Blue Parrot* (1953) and *National Lampoon's European Vacation* (1985).

Cambridge - University of Cambridge is one of the two most prominent universities in Great Britain. John Cleese attended Cambridge.

Cleveland, Carol - (Carol Cleveland; b. 1942) The (or a) seventh Python. She played more women's roles in Monty Python than any other actress.

Conoley, Terence - (1919 – 2016) An English actor who had roles in *A Fish Called Wanda* (1988) and *The Fall and Rise of Reginald Perrin* (1976 – 1977). In *A Touch of Class* he played Mr. Wareing. In *Waldorf Salad* he played Mr. Johnston.

Davies, John Howard - (1939 – 2011) Davies was a child actor who became well-known when he starred in *Oliver Twist* (1948). He became a successful producer and director and worked on *Monty Python's Flying Circus* and *Fawlty Towers*.

Dry sherry – In the UK, dry sherry is often associated with the upper class.

Ellis, Robin - (Anthony Robin Ellis; b. 1942) A British actor who played the part of Danny Brown in this episode. He was also in *Poldark* (1975 – 1977 and 2015 – 2019) and *The Case-Book of Sherlock Holmes* (1991).

Frost, David - (Sir David Paradine Frost; 1939 – 2013) Frost was a journalist, comedian and television presenter. He hired Graham Chapman (1941 – 1989), John Cleese, Eric Idle (b. 1943), Terry Jones (1942 – 2020) and Michael Palin (b. 1943) for *The Frost Report* which preceded Monty Python.

Gleneagles, Torquay – The Gleneagles in Torquay is the hotel where the Pythons stayed during one of their filmings. The hotel was the inspiration for *Fawlty Towers* and the manager, Donald Sinclair, formed the basis for the character Basil Fawlty.

Gwynn, Michael - (1916 – 1976) An English actor who played Lord Melbury in this episode. He also acted in several Hammer films.

Handkerchief up the sleeve – An aristocratic practice that is associated with British officers in World War I.

Lahr, Bert - (Irving Lahrheim; 1895 – 1967) Lahr was an actor and vaudeville performer best known for his role as the Cowardly Lion in *The Wizard of Oz* (1939).

Lahr, John - (John Henry Lahr; b. 1941) John Lahr was an American writer and theater critic. He is the son of Bert Lahr (Irving Lahrheim; 1895 – 1967) and has been married to Connie Booth since 2000.

Lord Melbury – The name comes from Melbury Road which was near where John Cleese lived.

Rockinghorse Winner, The – (1949) A fantasy film based on the short story by D. H. Lawrence (David Herbert Lawrence; 1885 – 1930). It stars a young John Howard Davies (1939 – 2011) among others. It is about a young boy who can pick racehorse winners with perfect accuracy.

Oliver Twist - (1948) A British film by Sir David Lean (1908 – 1991) based on the novel by Charles Dickens (Charles John Huffam Dickens; 1812 – 1870). The movie stars John Howard Davies (1939 – 2011) and Sir Alec Guinness (Alec Guinness de Cuffe; 1914 – 2000).

Simeon, David - (David John Townsend; b. 1943) A British actor who played Mr. Mackenzie in this episode. He also had parts in *Doctor Who* (1970 – 1971) and *A Fish Called Wanda* (1988).

Symons, Pat - Symons played Lady Morris in this episode although she is not credited. She was also in *The Invisible Man* (1959) and *Secret Agent* (1964).

Video Arts – A UK video training company for professionals. It was founded in 1972 by John Cleese (b. 1939) and Sir Antony Jay (Antony Rupert Jay; 1930 – 1916). The idea behind the company was to make entertaining videos to help people better learn the skills presented therein.

Wareing, Guy – (Capt. Guy Wilbraham Wareing; 1899 – 1918) A World War I flying ace in the Royal Flying Corps. He has been credited with nine aerial victories.

Wheeler, Lionel - (b. 1929) An English actor who played Mr. Watson in this episode. He was also in *The Avengers* (1968) and *Doctor in the House* (1969 – 1970).

Wilson, Dennis - (Dennis Miller Wilson; 1920 – 1989) Wilson composed the theme music for *Fawlty Towers*. He also composed the theme music for *Marriage Lines* (1961) and *Steptoe and Son* (1962).

Wyldeck, Martin - (1914 – 1988) He was an English actor who played Sir Richard Morris in this episode. He was also in *The Oblong Box* (1969) and *Die Screaming, Marianne* (1971).

Episode Two – The Builders

16 Elwood Avenue – The street address of Fawlty Towers.

Babbity-bumble – In this case "babbity-bumble" is probably just a sort of childish way of speaking. It is also a name from the story *The Tale of Mrs. Tittlemouse* (1910) by Beatrix Potter (Helen Beatrix Potter; 1866 – 1943).

Bangers – An informal British word for "sausages."

Bint – A British term that was added to the language during the occupation of Egypt. It means a "bit on the side" or "girlfriend."

Biscuit – A British term for a "cookie" or a "cracker."

Bit of gyp – A British term meaning "an uncomfortable amount of pain but nothing too serious."

Bloody – In Britain, it is a mildly impolite way of adding emphasis to what is being said.

Cloth-eared – A British way to describe someone who lacks the ability to appreciate music or the sound of words.

Compton, Denis - (Denis Charles Scott Compton; 1918 – 1997) A British cricketer and footballer. He is considered to have been one of the best bowlers in the history of cricket.

Cock-up artist – British term for "someone who is very good at messing things up."

Cowboy – British slang for "someone who is reckless or careless."

Cut-price – For sale at an unusually low price. In this case, it means a low price due to poor quality workmanship.

Dago – A derogatory term for a Spanish or Italian person.

Dance of the Sugar Plum Fairy – After Basil has O'Reilly "fix" the "repairs" he made; he plays *Dance of the Sugar Plum Fairy* on a tape deck to accompany Sybil's return to the hotel. The Sugar Plum fairy comes from *The Nutcracker* by Pyotr Ilyich Tchaikovsky (1840 – 1893).

Din-dins – A childlike way of saying "dinner."

Dustbins – British term for "garbage cans."

Garden gnome – Most people know what a garden gnome is. It is included here because on the LP version of the show Manuel calls in a "garden dwarf." The discrepancy is worth noting because the misnomer is rather amusing.

Garden wall – In the UK, a "yard" is called a "garden." A "garden wall" is "a wall that goes along the edge of the garden."

Genius of the lamp - This seems to be O'Reilly's way of saying "genie of the lamp." In the Three Stooges film *Three Arabian Nuts* (1951) there is a djinni of a magical lamp. The Stooges refer to the djinni as "genius."

Gleneagles - The Gleneagles in Torquay is the hotel where the Pythons stayed during one of their filmings. The hotel was the inspiration for *Fawlty Towers* and the manager, Donald Sinclair (Donald William Sinclair; 1909 – 1981), was the inspiration for Basil Fawlty.

Flick knife – Better known in the U. S. as a "switchblade." It is a knife that contains a spring-loaded blade in the handle.

Hadrian - (Caesar Trajanus Hadrianus; 76 CE – 138 CE) Hadrian was the Emperor of Rome from 117 CE to 138 CE. He is known for Hadrian's Wall which was built at the northern border of Britannia where it met Caledonia.

Half-wit – A stupid person.

Hoover - A brand of vacuum cleaner that has come to be synonymous with "vacuum cleaner."

Knuckle dusters – Brass knuckles.

Madrid – The capital city of Spain.

Paignton – One of three towns on Tor Bay in Devon that form the English Riviera. The other two towns are Brixham and Torquay.

Plebs – According to Oxford Languages, "pleb" is a derogatory term for "an ordinary person, especially one from the lower social classes."

Poor sod – An expression of sympathy for someone who is having a difficult time.

Soup tins – In the U. S. these would be called "soup cans."

Stubbs' critique of construction

>   **4x2** – A board that is two inches by four inches.

>   **Lintel** – According to Oxford Languages, a lintel is "a horizontal support of timber, stone, concrete, or steel across the top of a door or window."

>   **RSJ** – An abbreviation for "rolled steel joist." An RSJ is a steel beam with an H or I-shaped cross section. This form is used because it is good for carrying both shear and bending loads.

>   **Screw jack** – According to Oxford Languages, it is also known as a "jack screw" which is "a screw that can be turned to adjust the position of an object into which it fits."

>   **Supporting wall** - According to Oxford Languages, "Load-bearing walls support the weight of a floor or roof structure above and are so named because they can support a significant amount of weight. By contrast, a non-load-bearing wall, sometimes called a partition wall, is responsible only for holding up itself."

Ten paces – Ten paces is a distance that usually refers to how far each combatant must walk in a duel involving pistols.

Toxic midget – One of Basil's terms for Sybil. The term "midget" is considered derogatory because of its roots in freak shows from the 1800's. The first known usage of the word was in 1816.

Twit – According to Oxford Languages, a "twit" is "a silly or foolish person."

Spanish

Si - Yes

Quando nosotoras somos – When we are

De nada – You are welcome

Quiero subir para dormir – I want to go up to sleep. *Note: The subtitles on the DVD are different from the Spanish in the script. The subtitles show "Quiero ascender para dormir" and the meaning is basically the same.*

¿Qué? - What?

Si - Yes

Siesta - Nap

Señor O'Reilly - Mr. O'Reilly

Despiérteme - Wake me up

Subiré a tu cuarto a despertarte – I'll go up to your room to wake you up.

Antes que ellos comienzan a trabajar aqui, si? – Before they start working here, yes?

Comprendo - Understand

Generalissimo – The commander of a combined military force like the army, navy and air force. In this case the commander was Francisco Franco (Francisco Franco Bahamonde; 1892 – 1975).

From the commentary by John Cleese

Appleby, James - (1923 – 2004) Appleby played Stubbs in this episode. He also had roles in *Doctor Who* (1966 – 1976) and *Doctor at Sea* (1974).

Cronin, Michael - (b. 1942) Cronin played the part of Mr. Lurphy in this episode. He also had roles in *The Girl from Starship Venus* (1975) and *Naughty Girls on the Loose* (1976).

Devon accent – A dialect also called West Country English. The accent is similar to some American accents.

Dorman, Barney - (b. 1932) Dorman played Mr. Kerr in this episode. He also had roles in *Z Cars* (1975) and *Striker* (1976).

Fish Called Wanda, A - (1988) A comedy film written by John Cleese and Charles Crichton (Charles Ainslie Crichton; 1910 – 1999) and starring John Cleese, Michael Palin (Sir Michael Edward Palin; b. 1943), Jamie Lee Curtis (b. 1958) and Kevin Kline (Kevin Delaney Kline; b. 1947). It is a heist film featuring a barrister, femme fatale, and incompetent crooks.

Halsey, Michael - (1946 – 2017) An English actor who played Mr. Jones in this episode. He also had parts in *Blake's 7* (1978 – 1979) and *Are You Being Served?* (1978).

Horatio – Hamlet's friend from Shakespeare's (William Shakespeare; 1564 – 1616) play *The Tragedy of Hamlet, Prince of Denmark* (1599 – 1601).

Kelly, David - (1929 – 2012) An Irish actor who played Mr. O'Reilly in this episode. He is probably best known for his role in *Waking Ned* (1998), the American title of which is *Waking Ned Devine.*

Lee, George – A British actor who had roles in *Doctor Who* (1970 – 1972) and *Blake's 7* (1981). He played a delivery man in the *Fawlty Towers* episodes *The Builders* and *Communication Problems.*

Screen Actors Guild – An American union that represented actors, both principal and background or extra. In 2012 it merged with the American Federation of Television and Radio Artists and became SAG-AFTRA.

Wilson, Dennis - (Dennis Miller Wilson; 1920 – 1989) Wilson composed the theme music for *Fawlty Towers.* He also composed the theme music for *Marriage Lines* (1961) and *Steptoe and Son* (1962).

Episode Three – The Wedding Party

Barcelona – The largest city and capital of Catalonia which is an autonomous region of Spain.

Bellevue - There doesn't seem to be a Bellevue Hotel in Torquay. However, there have been some famous hotels of that name worldwide. In the 19th and 20th centuries there was the Grand Hotel Bellevue in Berlin. Until 1979, there was the Bellevue Hotel in Brisbane, Queensland, Australia. Still in existence today is the Hotel Bellevue Palace in the Old City of Bern, Switzerland. Finally, there is the Bellevue-Stratford Hotel in Philadelphia, Pennsylvania, USA.

Bless my soul – An idiomatic English phrase used to express surprise.

Blotto – Very drunk.

Bob's your uncle – A phrase used in the United Kingdom and Commonwealth countries to mean "there you have it."

By jove – An expression that is used to indicate surprise or to emphasize something.

Catering corp. - The British Army Catering Corps. (ACC) was formed in 1941 and was responsible for the feeding of all Army units. In 1993 it was combined with the Royal Logistics Corps.

Chemist – The British term for "pharmacist."

Chopin - (Frédéric François Chopin; b. Fryderyk Franciszek Chopin; 1810 - 1849) was a Polish composer and pianist. 230 of his works survive. The piece that is being played on the tape recorder when Mrs. Peignoir walks into the lobby is Nocturne in Db major, Op. 27/2.

Finishing school - According to Oxford Languages, a finishing school is "a private school where girls are prepared for entry into fashionable society."

Hobnob – To mix socially, especially with people of a higher class.

How to Murder Your Wife - (1965) An American black comedy movie directed by Richard Quine (1920 – 1989) and starring Jack Lemmon (John Uhler Lemmon III; 1925 – 2001) and Virna Lisi (Virna Lisa Pieralisi; 1936 – 2014).

Jaws (Basil is reading) - (1974) A novel by Peter Benchley (Peter Bradford Benchley; 1940 – 2006) about a great white shark attacking people in a resort town. The book is based on the exploits of shark fisherman Frank Mundus (1925 – 2008). The book was later adapted into a screenplay and directed by Steven Spielberg (Steven Allan Spielberg; b. 1946).

Kama Sutra – An ancient Sanskrit text attributed to the Indian philosopher Vātsyāyana during the second or third century CE. It is a guide to many things in life, but most famously to aspects of one's love life.

Keep your pecker up – A British idiom meaning "to stay cheerful."

Knocking shop – A brothel.

Korean War – A war fought between North and South Korea from 1950 to 1953. When North Korean forces entered South Korea, the United Nations Security Council authorized the formation of the United Nations Command that sent forces to Korea to repel the attack from North Korea.

Lord Byron – (George Gordon Byron, 6th Baron Byron; 1788 – 1824) was a Romantic poet and a peer of the United Kingdom. His best-known works include *Don Juan* (1819 - 1824) and *Childe Harold's Pilgrimage* (1812 – 1818). Byron fought against the Ottoman Empire during the Greek War of Independence. He died during that conflict.

Paint the town red – To go out on the town and enjoy oneself.

Peignoir – A light dressing gown or negligee.

Piece of cake – Refers to a task that is easy to do.

Ricard – A pastis created by Marseilles native Paul Ricard (Paul Louis Marius Ricard; 1909 – 1997) in 1932. It is an anise and licorice-flavored apéritif.

Sexy Laughs (Sybil is reading) - A saucy magazine from the 1970's. Each issue was filled with jokes and cartoons.

Singapore – The Republic of Singapore is an island country and city-state. It is located off the southern tip of the Malay Peninsula.

Sistine Chapel - A chapel in the Apostolic Palace, residence of the pope, in Vatican City. Michelangelo

28

painted the ceiling between 1508 and 1512 under the orders of Pope Julius II (Giuliano della Rovere; 1443 – 1513).

Sponge cake – In the UK, a sponge cake is a type of cake made with flour, sugar, egg whites and sometimes baking powder. The oldest known recipe for sponge cake, also known as biscuit bread, is from Gervase Markham's (1568 - 1637) *The English Huswife, Containing the Inward and Outward Virtues which Ought to Be in a Compleat Woman* (1615).

Tart – According to Oxford Languages, a "tart" is "a woman who dresses or behaves in a way that is considered tasteless and sexually provocative."

Vat 69 – This is probably just a random prop used to fill out the bar. Vat 69 is a blended Scotch whisky.

French:

> **Enchanté** - Delighted to meet you.
>
> **Bonne nuit** – Good night
>
> **Dormez bien** – Sleep well
>
> **Et maintenant, un peu de café?** - And now, some coffee?
>
> **Café au lait** – Coffee with milk.
>
> **Voilà sommes nous** - *Nonsense by someone who doesn't speak French.*

Café pour vous – Coffee for you (plural or formal).

Pas pour toi? - Not for you? (singular or informal).

Bonne nuit – Good night

Au naturel – Sleeping in the nude.

Spanish:

¿Qué? - What?

He creduto que – I have believed that.

Olé - An expression of excitement or joy.

Si – Yes

Siesta – Nap

From the commentary by John Cleese

Adams, Trevor - (Trevor Michael Adams; 1946 – 2000) A British actor who plays Alan in this episode. He had roles in *The Rise and Rise of Reginald Perrin* (1976 – 1979) and *The New Avengers* (1977).

Aitken, Maria - (Maria Penelope Katherine Aitken; b. 1945) She is an actress who played the part of Wendy Leach in *A Fish Called Wanda* (1988).

Chew the scenery – To overact.

Climbdown – A retreat from an earlier position in a negotiation or an argument.

Davies, John Howard - (1939 – 2011) Davies was a child actor who became well-known when he starred in *Oliver Twist* (1948). He became a successful producer and director and worked on *Monty Python's Flying Circus* and *Fawlty Towers*.

Fish Called Wanda, A - (1988) A comedy film written by John Cleese and Charles Crichton (Charles Ainslie Crichton; 1910 – 1999) and starring John Cleese, Michael Palin (Sir Michael Edward Palin; b. 1943), Jamie Lee Curtis (b. 1958) and Kevin Kline (Kevin Delaney Kline; b. 1947). It is a heist film featuring a barrister, femme fatale, and incompetent crooks.

Gilan, Yvonne - (Yvonne Janette Gilan; 1931 – 2018) A Scottish actress who plays Mrs. Peignoir in this episode. She was also in *Chariots of Fire* (1981) and *Empire of the Sun* (1987).

King, Diana - (1918 – 1986) An English actress who played Mrs. Lloyd in this episode. She was also in *The Avengers* (1961) and *Pink Floyd – The Wall* (1980).

Phillips, Conrad - (Conrad Philip Havord; 1925 – 2016) An English screen actor who played Mr. Lloyd in this episode. He also played parts in *The Avengers* (1966) and *The Prisoner* (1967).

Presbyterian – Part of the Reformed tradition within Protestantism that can be traced back to Scotland. According to John Cleese, a Presbyterian is "someone who has a nasty suspicion that somebody, somewhere might be enjoying themselves."

31

Walker, April - (b. 1943) A British actress who played the part of Jean Wilson in this episode. She was also in *The Two Ronnies* (1973 – 1984) and she was cast as Sarah Jane Smith on *Doctor Who* but was not used because Jon Pertwee preferred Elisabeth Sladen (1946 – 2011).

Wickets – According to Oxford Languages, wickets in cricket are "each of the sets of three stumps with two bails across the top at either end of the pitch, defended by a batsman."

Aloxe-Corton – A type of wine made in the Aloxe-Corton commune in France.

Barcelona - The largest city and capital of Catalonia which is an autonomous region of Spain.

BBC2 – A public broadcast television service. It airs programs of more depth and substance than the mainstream BBC1.

Blackfoot Indians – A group of Native Americans that make up the Blackfoot Confederacy. They were a group of people related linguistically. They were also nomadic bison hunters in the Great Plains of North America.

Body – Full of flavor in reference to wine.

Bordeaux - Wine from the Bordeaux region in the southwest of France.

Borstal – A detention center for youths in the United Kingdom and Commonwealth countries.

Brylcreem - A British brand of hair styling products. Founded in 1928 in Birmingham, England.

Claremont – This is supposed to be the name of another hotel in Torquay. Such a hotel does not seem to exist. The closest match is the Claremont country house in Esher, Surrey, England which is roughly 170 miles (274 kilometers) from Torquay.

Claret - A type of red wine in the style of a Bordeaux.

33

Corked – Corked wine is a wine that has been contaminated with cork taint. This happens when wine is bottled with a cork that is contaminated with Trichloroanisole (TCA).

Duke of Kent – A peerage title that has been created multiple times in Great Britain and the United Kingdom. The title is currently held by Prince Edward (Edward George Nicholas Paul Patrick; b. 1935) who is first cousins with Queen Elizabeth II (Elizabeth Alexandra Mary; 1926 – 2022).

Elephant's ear – A crispy, fried cinnamon-sugar bread.

Give him one – Although "give him one" is often used as an idiom for "to have sex with someone," in this context it more probably means "to give him a punch."

In a nutshell – A summary of something in the fewest possible words.

Kissinger, Henry - (Henry Alfred Kissinger, b. Heinz Alfred Kissinger; 1923) A Jewish refugee from Nazi Germany best known for being Secretary of State under American presidents Richard Nixon (Richard Milhous Nixon; 1913 – 1994) and Gerald Ford (Gerald Rudolph Ford, Jr., b. Leslie Lynch King, Jr.; 1913 – 2006).

Morton, Bill – Named after the vision mixer for *Fawlty Towers*.

Outboard motor – According to Merriam-Webster, an outboard motor is "a small internal combustion engine with propeller integrally attached for mounting at the stern of a small boat."

Pâté Maison – A liver pâté made from chicken livers and pork sausage wrapped in bacon.

Penny's dropped - "The penny has dropped" means that someone has finally understood something. The expression refers to the old penny-in-the-slot machines.

Prawn cocktail – Also known as shrimp cocktail, this is a dish served in a glass with prawns and cocktail sauce.

Saber-toothed tart – One of Basil's terms of endearment for Sybil. "Saber-tooth" probably refers to a saber-toothed tiger or any one of the saber-toothed carnivorous mammals from the Eocene (56 million – 33.9 million years ago) and Pleistocene (approx. 2.58 million – 11,700 years ago) eras. According to Oxford Languages, a tart is "a woman who dresses or behaves in a way that is considered tasteless and sexually provocative."

Spanish omelette – A traditional Spanish dish also called a Spanish tortilla. It is made with eggs and potatoes and sometimes onion. Some people insist that fresh peas are an integral part of the dish.

Squawking Bird – There is no record of a Squawking Bird.

Whit - "It matters not one whit" meaning that something does not matter one iota.

Yobbo – A British way of saying a "yokel" or a "lout."

Spanish:

Come se habla en Ingles pero puedo ver las nombres solamente quando estan delante de mi - As spoken in English but I can see the names only when they are in front of me.

Señor - Mister

Adios – Goodbye

From the commentary by John Cleese

Brett, Peter - (b. 1940) Brett played the part of Brian, the first hotel inspector, in this episode. He was also in *Monty Python's Life of Brian* (1979) and is the ex-husband of Carol Cleveland (b. 1942).

Cossins, James - (1933- 1997) Cossins played Mr. Walt in this episode. He was an English character actor who also had roles in *How I Won the War* (1967) and *The Rise and Rise of Michael Rimmer* (1970).

Cribbins, Bernard - (Bernard Joseph Cribbins; 1928 – 2022) Cribbins was an English actor and singer who played the part of Mr. Hutchinson in this episode. He made the novelty record *Right Said Fred* (1962) and was in *Frenzy* (1972) and *Doctor Who* (2007 – 2010).

Fish Called Wanda, A - (1988) A comedy film written by John Cleese and Charles Crichton (Charles Ainslie Crichton; 1910 – 1999) and starring John Cleese, Michael Palin (Sir Michael Edward Palin; b. 1943), Jamie Lee Curtis (b. 1958) and Kevin Kline (Kevin Delaney Kline; b. 1947). It is a heist film featuring a barrister, femme fatale, and incompetent crooks.

36

Hutchinson, Alan – Mr. Hutchinson is named after Alan Hutchinson, the oldest friend of John Cleese from Cambridge. The name is also used in a sketch by John Cleese and Graham Chapman (1941 – 1989) called *A Bed-time Book* which appears on *Monty Python's Previous Record* (1972).

Sherman, Polly – Named after Pipper Sherman who was the godmother of John and Connie's daughter, Cynthia.

Walt, Nicholas – Mr. Walt was named after Mr. Nicholas Walt who was the proprietor of an artists' materials shop in Covent Garden. He was a good friend of John Cleese.

Amphibious landing craft – A light military boat that transported troops from a ship to the shore as part of an invasion. They are generally associated with WWII.

Brown ale – A type of beer with brown or dark amber color.

Burst his zip – Popped his zipper apart.

Carrier, Robert - (Robert Carrier McMahon; 1923 – 2006) A famous American chef and restaurateur who found success and spent most of his career in the United Kingdom.

Chablis – Wine that comes from Chablis which is in the Burgundy region of France.

Chips – The British term for "French fries."

Culinary soiree – An evening gathering for food and conversation.

Echo, The – *The Echo* is a daily newspaper in South Essex, England.

"There's a hair in my mousse." - To which Polly replies, "Well, don't talk too loud or everybody will want one." This is a variation on an old joke that begins with, "Waiter, there's a fly in my soup," the responses to which are various.

Hauté cuisine – According to Oxford Languages, hauté cuisine is "the preparation and cooking of high-quality food following the style of traditional French cuisine" or "high-quality food in the style of traditional French cuisine."

I Cain't Say No – A song by Richard Rodgers (Richard Charles Rodgers; 1902 – 1979) and Oscar Hammerstein II (Oscar Greeley Clendenning Hammerstein II; 1895 – 1960). It was part of the 1943 musical play *Oklahoma!*

J. P.'s - Justices of the peace also known as magistrates. These judges dispense summary justice. There are often three magistrates on the bench in one court.

Kissinger, Henry - (Henry Alfred Kissinger, b. Heinz Alfred Kissinger; 1923) A Jewish refugee from Nazi Germany best known for being Secretary of State under American presidents Richard Nixon (Richard Milhous Nixon; 1913 – 1994) and Gerald Ford (Gerald Rudolph Ford, Jr., b. Leslie Lynch King, Jr.; 1913 – 2006).

Mickey Mouse - A cartoon mouse who was co-created in 1928 by Walt Disney (Walter Elias Disney; 1901 – 1966) and Ub Iwerks (Ubbe Ert Iwwerks; 1901 – 1971). Mickey Mouse is the mascot of The Walt Disney Company.

Mousse – A prepared food that is light and airy due to the bubbles that are added for texture.

Mullet – Mullets are a kind of fish that comprise a family of ray-finned fish. They are found in coastal temperate and tropical waters.

Paella – The name "paella" comes from the Valencian word for frying pan. The principal ingredients are rice, chicken, rabbit, vegetables, green beans, lima beans and saffron.

Potted shrimps – A British dish made with brown shrimp, nutmeg and butter, which acts as a preservative. Cayenne pepper is sometimes added, and the dish is often eaten with bread.

Proles – A working class person; a member of the proletariat.

Pulitzer Prize - Awards created by the will of Joseph Pulitzer (b. Pulitzer József; 1847 - 1911) in 1917. They recognize excellence in journalism, creative writing and music composition.

Riffraff – According to Oxford Languages, "riffraff" refers to "disreputable or undesirable people."

Rotarian - A member of Rotary International, a service organization bringing together business and professional leaders to provide humanitarian service.

Salad cream – A condiment containing water, oil, egg yolk and vinegar. It is similar to mayonnaise.

Sauced – Intoxicated or drunk. The word may be a mixture of "soused" and "sauce," which can mean liquor.

Smarties-shaped – In the United Kingdom, Smarties are a type of candy made with milk chocolate. "Smarties-shaped" would probably mean disc-shaped.

Smashed eggs – The British way of saying "scrambled eggs."

Tournedos – According to Oxford Languages, a tournedos is *"a small round thick cut from a fillet of beef."*

Trifle – According to Oxford Languages, a trifle is *"a cold dessert of sponge cake and fruit covered with layers of custard, jelly, and cream."*

van Gogh, Vincent - (Vincent Willem van Gogh; 1853 – 1890) A Dutch Post-Impressionist painter who battled extreme poverty and mental illness. While he was not financially successful during his lifetime, his work has been highly influential in the western art world.

Watney's Red Barrel - Another visual reference. It is likely just what the prop department chose to place in the set. Watney's Red Barrel is a bitter sold in the United Kingdom and especially popular during the 1960s and 1970s. Brewed by Watney Combe & Reid in London.

Win a bun – Presumably, Basil would like to know if guessing the subject of the drawing would win someone a small, fairly worthless prize.

French:

> **Au fait** – Can mean "by the way" or "up to speed, on top of things." In this context, it means the latter.

Spanish:

> **¿Qué?** - What?

Famoso - Famous

From the commentary by John Cleese

294 Preston Rd., Harrow - The location of where Andrés Restaurant was created for the show. A Torquay telephone number was added to make it seem like it was in Torquay.

Austin 1300 Estate – The make and model of the car that receives a "damn good thrashing."

Benson, Elizabeth - (b. 1926) Benson played Mrs. Heath in *Gourmet Night* and Mrs. White in *The Kipper and the Corpse*. She was also in *Dr. Finlay's Casebook* (1967) and *The Agatha Christie Hour* (1982).

Caldicot, Richard - (1908 – 1995) Caldicot played Lionel Twitchen in this episode. He is known for his voice acting on the BBC radio series *The Navy Lark* (1959 – 1977).

***Clockwise* -** (1986) A British comedy film starring John Cleese, written by Michael Frayn (b. 1933) and directed by Christopher Morahan (Christopher Thomas Morahan; 1929 – 2017). It is a comedy about a headmaster who is obsessed with punctuality. He finds himself in a dilemma where he must fight to not be late for a Headmasters' Conference.

Cooster – The surname of a couple who John Cleese and Connie Booth knew. The couple was invited to dinner and cancelled at the last moment. Therefore, they decided to name of the couple who cancelled dinner in the show "Cooster."

Frayn, Michael – (b. 1933) The director of the movie *Clockwise* (1986) starring John Cleese.

Huntley-Wright, Betty - (1911 – 1993) Huntley-Wright played Mrs. Twitchen in this episode. She played parts in *The Last Waltz* (1936) and *Carry On Loving* (1970).

Maranne, André - (1926 – 2021) Maranne played the part of André in this episode. He is known for playing the part of Sgt. François Chevalier in six of the Pink Panther films.

Page, Tony – Page played the part of Ronald Heath in this episode. He went on to have his own catering business.

Plonky - Clumsy or cheap and inferior.

Plytas, Steve - (Phokion Stavros Plytas; 1913 – 1994) He played Kurt in this episode. He also played parts in *The Avengers* (1963 – 1966) and *Doctor Who* (1966).

Segal, Jeffrey - (1920 – 2015) In this episode, Segal played Mr. Heath. He was also in the shows *UFO* (1970) and *Doctor At Large* (1971).

Steadman, Alison - (b. 1946) She is an English actress who has been in *A Private Function* (1984) and *Clockwise* (1986).

Way, Ann - (1915 – 1993) In this episode she played Mrs. Hall, the diminutive wife of the Colonel. She was an English character actress and she also worked with Cleese on the movie *Clockwise* (1986).

Technical talk

Cut away – An interruption of a shot of a subject to show something different. Often there is then a return to the first shot.

Reaction shot – A shot that is cut away from the main action or dialogue to show a character's reaction.

Take it down – This generally refers to reducing the intensity of a situation or the lines being spoken.

Tight shot – A close up in which the camera seems very near the subject.

Timing – How long something takes. For example, in comedy it often refers to the amount of time between the lines of two different characters.

Wide shot – A shot that shows all of the main object or person and the surrounding area in a frame.

"A blow on the head like that is worth two in the bush." - When Basil says this, he is mixed up because of the blow he has suffered to the head. He seems lost about halfway through the sentence and ends with the second half of the old saying "a bird in the hand is worth two in the bush."

Admirable Crichton, The – Originally a play (1902) by J. M. Barrie (Sir James Matthew Barrie, 1st Baronet; 1860 – 1937) before being made into a film on four occasions (1918, 1950, 1957, 1968) and a radio play (2011). The story is about a group of aristocrats who, along with the butler, Crichton, get stranded on an island. The only one in the group with sufficient survival skills is Crichton. It is interesting that Basil Fawlty compares Manuel to Crichton. Although Manuel is a well-meaning employee he is seen as incompetent due to his lack of understanding which is, of course, rooted in his lack of English language skills.

Bed jacket – A light jacket that goes over bed clothes. It is generally worn to cover the chest, arms and shoulders while a person is sitting upright in bed.

Berlin – The capital of Germany.

Bloody - In Britain, it is a mildly impolite way of adding emphasis to what is being said.

By jove - An expression that is used to indicate surprise or to emphasize something.

Cagney, Jimmy ("You dirty rat") - (James Francis Cagney, Jr.; 1899 – 1986) An American entertainer best known for acting in movies. Often, he played a tough guy as in *The Public Enemy* (1932), *Angels With Dirty Faces* (1938) and *White Heat* (1949). Cagney never actually said the line "You dirty rat," but he did utter "Yellow bellied rat," in the movie *Taxi* (1931).

Cardies - Cardigan sweaters.

Colditz salads – This is a play on cold meat salads and the Colditz Castle which was a prisoner of war camp used by the Germans during World War II.

Eggs mayonnaise – A food made with chopped eggs and mayonnaise. In the U. S. it would be called "egg salad."

German invasion of Poland – Germany invaded Poland on September 1, 1939. Many people consider this the official beginning of World War II.

German sense of humor – Germans are notorious for not having much of a sense of humor, at least since World War II. One reason is that the Nazis sent the Jewish entertainers to concentration camps. The non-Jewish comedians generally refused to perform during the Third Reich.

Goebbels, Joseph - (Paul Joseph Goebbels; 1897 – 1945) He was the Reich Minister of Propaganda for Nazi Germany.

Goering, Hermann - (Hermann Wilhelm Göring; 1893 – 1946) Goering was a Minister Without Portfolio in the Nazi German government.

Hampshire – Hampshire County Cricket Club, which is one of eighteen first-class county clubs in England and Wales.

Himmler, Heinrich - (Heinrich Luitpold Himmler; 1900 – 1945) Himmler was a leading member of the Nazi Party and the primary architect of the Holocaust.

Hitler, Adolf - (1889 – 1945) Hitler was the leader of the Nazi Party.

Hundredweight – A hundredweight differs between the American and British systems of measurement. The U. S. hundredweight, also called the short or central hundredweight, is equal to 100 pounds (45.36 kilograms). The British hundredweight, also called the long or imperial hundredweight, is equal 8 stone or 112 pounds (50.8 kilograms).

India – The national cricket team of India.

Korean War - A war fought between North and South Korea from 1950 to 1953. When North Korean forces entered South Korea, the United Nations Security Council authorized the formation of the United Nations Command that sent forces to Korea to repel the attack from North Korea.

Kraut - A derogatory term for Germans.

Lime cream – A type of lime candy that is often covered with chocolate or white chocolate.

Minds like Swiss cheese – Meaning that their minds seemingly have holes in them. Swiss cheese is most readily identifiable by the holes caused by tiny bits of hay that get into the cheese during the manufacture.

Northwick Park Hospital (sign) - At the beginning of the episode, this sign is visible outside the hospital. The hospital itself is in real life located in Harrow, North West London. A drive between Torquay and London in light traffic would generally take three and a half hours. There are hospitals in and near Torquay. Probably the Northwick Park Hospital was what they had available when they did location shooting.

Oh, Buddha - Probably just a variation of "Oh, God."

Oval, The - An international cricket ground in Kennington in the London Borough of Lambeth, in south London.

Piano wire – Also called "music wire," piano wire is a type of thin wire with a high tensile strength. It is used in making strings for pianos and other musical instruments. It also has applications in other areas like special effects for movies.

Pickled herring - A popular type of preserved fish in Europe.

Plaice - A type of North Atlantic flatfish.

Prawn cocktail - Also known as shrimp cocktail, this is a dish served in a glass with prawns and cocktail sauce.

Prawn, Eva – A mashup of a type of shrimp and Eva Braun (Eva Anna Paula Hitler, née Braun, 1912 – 1945). Braun was the longtime girlfriend of Adolf Hitler (1889 – 1945) and briefly his wife.

Scream – In this context, "scream" means a "humorous thing or situation."

Semitone – According to Oxford Languages, a semitone is "the smallest interval used in classical Western music, equal to a twelfth of an octave or half a tone. Also called a half step."

Sister – According to Oxford Languages, in British English a "sister" is "a senior female nurse, typically in charge of a ward."

Sod - In the UK, "poor sod" means someone who is to be felt sorry for.

Surrey – A county in Southeast England.

Von Ribbentrop, Joachim - (Ulrich Friedrich Wilhelm Joachim von Ribbentrop; 1893 – 1946) He was Foreign Minister of Nazi Germany.

Wall plug – According to Oxford Languages, a "wall plug" is "a fiber or plastic dowel inserted into a drilled hole to provide a gripping base for a screw."

War, The – World War II.

West Indians – Inhabitants of the West Indies. The West Indies are a chain of islands between Florida and South America.

Wilde, Oscar - (Oscar Fingal O'Flahertie Wills Wilde; 1854 – 1900) was an Irish writer. Best known for *The Importance of Being Earnest* (1895) and *The Picture of Dorian Gray* (1890).

Wilson, Harold - (James Harold Wilson, Baron Wilson of Rievaulx; 1916 – 1995) He was Prime Minister of the United Kingdom (1964 – 1970 and 1974 – 1976) and Leader of the Labour Party (1963 – 1976).

Wog - A derogatory term used in British English to mean anyone who is not white.

French:

    Au revoir – Goodbye

German:

    Bitte - Please

    Bitte schön - You are welcome.

    Ein bisschen. - A little.

    Entschuldigen Sie bitte, können Sie Deutsch sprechen? - Excuse me, can you speak German?

    Gnädiges Fräulein, können Sie mir sagen, wann das Mittagsessen serviert wird bitte? - Madam, can you tell me when lunch is served, please?

    Sprechen Sie Deutsch? - Do you speak German?

    Um ein Uhr. Fünf Minuten. - At one o'clock. Five minutes.

Vielen Dank – Many thanks.

Wir wollen ein Auto mieten. - We want to rent a car.

Wunderbar – Wonderful

Spanish:

¿Cómo? - How?

¿Qué? - What?

Fuego - Fire

De nada – You are welcome.

From the commentary by John Cleese

Bank Dick, The - (1940) A comedy film by W. C. Fields (William Claude Dukenfield; 1880 – 1946), considered by many people to be his best work. The author, however, believes that *It's a Gift* (1934) is Fields' funniest film.

Bergmayr, Lisa - (1915 – 1993) An English actress who had roles in *Doctor Who* (1977) and Crossroads (1967 – 1978). In this episode she played the German guest who gets upset and places her head on the table.

Bomphray, Ken – One of the visual effects artists on Fawlty Towers. He also worked on *7 of 1* (1973) and *Doctor Who* (1976).

Bowman, Willy - (1915 – 2002) A German actor who had roles in *Doctor Who* (1970 – 1976) and *The New*

Avengers (1976). He played one of the German guests in this episode.

Cotton, Bill – (Sir William Frederick Cotton; 1928 – 2008) The BBC head of Light Entertainment.

Fields, W. C. - (William Claude Dukenfield; 1880 – 1946) Fields was a comedy writer and performer. His characters were generally known as henpecked husbands who suffered from alcoholism and disliked dogs and children. He worked with other famous comics like Mae West (Mary Jane "Mae" West; 1893 – 1980) and Stooge Shemp Howard (Samuel Horwitz; 1895 – 1955). Fields is best known for *The Bank Dick* (1940) which had a large budget and some elaborate chase scenes.

Kane, Nick – An actor who also had a role in *Crime and Punishment* (1979). He played one of the German guests in this episode.

Lawrence, John – An actor who had roles in *Doctor Who* (1966) and *Virgin of the Secret Service* (1968). In this episode he played Mr. Sharp.

Mahoney, Louis - (Louis Felix Danner Mahoney; 1938 – 2020) A Gambian-born British actor who played parts in *Live and Let Die* (1973) and *General Hospital* (1976 – 1979). He was the physician in this episode.

One beat – The smallest unit of action in a play.

Pegrum, Peter – He worked on the visual effects for *Fawlty Towers*. He also worked on *Blake's 7* (1979) and *Doctor Who* (1971 – 1983).

Plonky – Clumsy or cheap and inferior.

Rix, Brian- (Brian Norman Roger Rix, Baron Rix; 1924 – 2016) Rix was an English stage actor, manager and producer. He had tremendous success producing farces for the London stage.

Speight, Johnny - (1920 – 1998) Speight was a television writer. He wrote for Morecambe (John Eric "Eric Morecambe" Bartholomew; 1926 – 1984) & Wise (Ernest "Ernie Wise" Wiseman; 1925 – 1999) and Peter Sellers (Richard Henry Sellers; 1925 – 1980). Speight is perhaps best known for creating the character Alf Garnett, a bigot on the show *Till Death Do Us Part* (1965 – 1975).

Till Death Do Us Part - (1965 – 1975) A British sitcom created by Johnny Speight (1920 – 1998). It is centered around Alf Garnett, a reactionary, racist white man who is working class and opposed to socialism. Garnett's daughter, Rita Rawlins, was portrayed by Una Stubbs (1937 – 2021). Stubbs also played Alice in the *Fawlty Towers* episode *The Anniversary*.

Whitehall farces – A series of farces that were produced for the Whitehall Theatre in London's West End. The theatre is currently called Trafalgar Theatre.

Atwell, Winnie - (Una Winifred Atwell; 1910 or 1914
– 1983) A pianist from Trinidad who had several
boogie-woogie and ragtime hits. She was very popular
in Great Britain and Australia during the 1950s. She
made history by being the first Black woman to have a
number one hit on the charts in the United Kingdom.

Barcelona - The largest city and capital of Catalonia
which is an autonomous region of Spain.

Bin - The British term for "trash container."

Birdbrain - According to Oxford Languages,
"birdbrain" means "an annoyingly stupid and shallow
person."

Brenda – From what Sybil says, Brenda is probably
someone who is supposed to start working as a maid at
Fawlty Towers the following Monday.

Brighton - A seaside resort in East Sussex, on the coast
of England.

Buttery – According to L'Oréal Paris, "Buttery blonde
hair is a warm, natural-looking blonde hair color. It
features a medium blonde base with a mix of both
warm and cool-toned blonde highlights resulting in a
mane that's full of movement. Butter can come in
varying shades: a sunny yellow, subtle cream, and even
the toasted brown from the bottom of a slightly burned
pan. Now, envision this medley of dimensional buttery
hues blended on your own head! Each shade can be

emphasized or played down depending on the look you're going for, making the blonde hair color totally customizable."

Caan, James - (James Edmund Caan; 1940 – 2022) Caan was a famous American film actor perhaps best known for playing Sonny Corleone in *The Godfather* (1972) and *The Godfather Part II* (1974).

Cavaliera rusticana - (1890) A one act opera by Pietro Mascagni (1863 – 1945) with an Italian libretto by Giovanni Targioni-Tozzetti (1863 – 1934) and Guido Menasci (1867 – 1925). It is based on the 1880 short story of the same name by Giovanni Verga (Giovanni Carmelo Verga di Fontanabianca; 1840 – 1922).

Cosmopolitan - A fashion and entertainment magazine for women published in the U. S. It began as a family magazine in 1886, became a literary magazine and, in 1965, transformed into a women's magazine. The issue that Sybil is looking at is from July 1972. The article with Burt Reynolds (Burton Leon Reynolds, Jr.; 1936 – 2018) and James Caan (James Edmund Caan; 1940 – 2022) is called *"So It's a Bracelet. What's It to Ya?"* by Robert L. Green (c. 1922 – 1997). The photographs are by Pete Turner (Donald Peter Turner; 1934 – 2017) and Victor Skrebneski (Victor Paul Skrebneski; (1929 – 2020).

De Camptown Races – Also known as *Gwine to Run All Night* (published in 1850) was a minstrel song by Stephen Foster (Stephen Collins Foster; 1826 – 1864).

Exeter – The Devon and Exeter racecourse now known as the Exeter racecourse. It is known locally as the Haldon racecourse due to the fact that it rests on the

Haldon Hills. Horse racing has been taking place in Exeter since the middle of the seventeenth century.

Filly - A female horse that is less than four years old.

Flutter – An informal British term meaning "a small bet."

Gee-gee – A British term used by children and in betting that means "a horse."

Glendower St. - The name of an actual street in Torquay.

Hanging Gardens of Babylon – One of the seven wonders of the ancient world, the hanging gardens were located near what is now Hillah, Bibal Province, Iraq. It was considered an amazing feat of engineering.

Krakatoa – A volcano located between the islands of Java and Sumatra in Indonesia. In August of 1883, the eruptions of Krakatoa were the most violent volcanic eruptions in recorded history.

Lavatory paper – A British term for "toilet paper."

Leisure Complex – A song by Dave Gold and Gordon Rees performed by the European Sound Stage Orchestra. This composition is playing on the radio when Basil is testing it for Mrs. Richards in her room.

Loo paper – A British term for "toilet paper."

My Way - A song with music from the French song *Comme d'habitude* by French composers Claude François (Claude Antoine Marie François; 1939 –

1978) and Jacques Revaux (b. Jacques Abel Jules Revaud; b. 1940) and lyrics by Paul Anka (Paul Albert Anka; b. 1941). It was made popular in 1969 by Frank Sinatra (Francis Albert Sinatra; 1915 – 1998).

Nell Gwyn - (Eleanor Gwyn, spelled variously as Gwynn or Gwynne; (1650 – 1687) Known for being one of the first actresses on the English stage and as a mistress of King Charles II of England, Scotland and Ireland (1630 – 1685).

Pansy – A derogatory term for a "homosexual."

"Pay the tax on it before…" - When betting on horses in Great Britain, one can pay tax on the stake and not have to pay tax again on the winnings.

Quid - British slang for "pound sterling."

Reynolds, Burt - (Burton Leon Reynolds, Jr.; 1936 – 2018) An American actor, director and sex symbol, Reynolds had his breakthrough moment when he starred in the movie *Deliverance* (1972).

Richards, Alice – According to the commentary by Cleese, this character was named by Connie Booth. Booth's exact reason for choosing the name is unknown.

Samaritans, The – An ethnoreligious group that is descended from the ancient Israelites. According to Luke 10:33, Samaritans are both helpful and charitable people.

Sinatra, Frank - (Francis Albert Sinatra; 1915 – 1998) Sinatra was an American singer, actor and producer. He sold more than 150 million records worldwide.

Spruce – Dressed very neatly.

St. George's Day – The feast day of Saint George, England's patron saint. It falls on April 23. Saint George, also known as George of Lydda (d. 303 CE). He is perhaps best known for the legend of Saint George and the Dragon.

Sun, The – A British tabloid newspaper owned by Rupert Murdoch (Keith Rupert Murdoch; b. 1931). Unknown whether it was chosen for the Major to read due to some significance or if it was randomly chosen by the props department.

Swanage – A coastal town in Dorset. According to the Cleese commentary it was picked simply because it's a funny name.

Sydney Opera House - A performing arts center at Sydney Harbor in Sydney, New South Wales, Australia. It is known for its distinct architecture.

Teatime – A time in the afternoon when tea is served.

Topaz – A dark yellow. The color comes from the gem topaz.

Torquay - A seaside resort town in Devon, England.

Trouble and strife – Cockney rhyming slang for "wife."

V. A. T. - Value-added tax, a type of tax that is based on the value of a product at each stage of production, distribution and sale.

Warning off – Telling someone to stay away because of danger.

Watney's Red Barrel - Another visual reference. It is probably just what the prop department chose to place in the set. Watney's Red Barrel is a bitter sold in the United Kingdom and especially popular during the 1960s and 1970s. Brewed by Watney, Combe and Reid in London.

Whip round – According to dictionary dot com, "whip round" is a primarily British term that refers to "an impromptu collection of money."

Winnie – According to John Cleese, "Winnie" refers to Winston Churchill (Sir Winston Leonard Spencer-Churchill; 1874 – 1965) in this instance. Churchill was Prime Minister of the United Kingdom during World War II.

You Make Me Feel So Young – A 1946 popular song by Josef Myrow (1910 – 1987) and Mack Gordon (b. Morris Glitter; 1904 – 1959). In 1956 the song was recorded by Frank Sinatra (Francis Albert Sinatra; 1915 – 1998).

Spanish

¿Qué? - What?

Si - Yes

Muchos - Many

From the commentary by John Cleese

Aberdeen – A coastal city in North East Scotland.

Argent, Douglas - (Douglas George Charles Argent; 1921 – 2010) He was an English producer and director. Besides *Fawlty Towers* he worked on *Steptoe and Son* (1974) and *EastEnders* (1991).

Back cloth – A cloth (often painted) in the back of a stage to provide scenery.

Cockney - An English dialect and accent spoken primarily in the East End of London by the working-class and the lower middle-class.

Davies, John Howard - (1939 – 2011) Davies was a child actor who became well-known when he starred in *Oliver Twist* (1948). He became a successful producer and director and worked on *Monty Python's Flying Circus* and *Fawlty Towers*.

Die in harness – An idiomatic term meaning to die while still actively working or being able to work.

Dublin accent – The Dublin accent is the way the residents of Dublin pronounce Dublin English. There are at least two Dublin accents, North Dublin and South Dublin. Dublin English is the Hiberno-English, aka Irish English, fka Anglo-Irish.

Farce – According to Oxford Languages, a "farce" is "a comic dramatic work using buffoonery and horseplay and typically including crude characterization and ludicrously improbable situations." Cleese has described *Fawlty Towers* as a French farce, where a small lie is told to cover up a situation and then more and more lies must be told to make the first lie plausible.

Fish Called Wanda, A - (1988) A comedy film written by John Cleese and Charles Crichton (Charles Ainslie Crichton; 1910 – 1999) and starring John Cleese, Michael Palin (Sir Michael Edward Palin; b. 1943), Jamie Lee Curtis (b. 1958) and Kevin Kline (Kevin Delaney Kline; b. 1947). It is a heist film featuring a barrister, femme fatale, and incompetent crooks.

Glass Menagerie, The - (1944) A memory play by Tennessee Williams (Thomas Lanier Williams, III; 1911 – 1983). It is a semi-autobiographical play. It is also the one that boosted Williams' career as a playwright, making him a star.

Goleman, Daniel – (b. 1946) is an American psychologist and author. He wrote a bestselling book called *Emotional Intelligence* (1995). One of the key points in the book is that stress can make a person stupid.

Hall, Brian - (Brian Charles Hall; 1937 – 1997) He was added as a regular to the cast for the second series of *Fawlty Towers* in the role of Terry Hughes. Hall also had roles in *Up the Elephant and Round the Castle* (1983) and *The Grass Arena* (1991).

Lankesheer, Robert - (1914 – 1993) He was a British actor who was known for roles in *The Dales* (1963 – 1966) and *Doctor Who* (1965).

Lee, George – A British actor who had roles in *Doctor Who* (1970 – 1972) and *Blake's 7* (1981). He played a delivery man in the *Fawlty Towers* episodes *The Builders* and *Communication Problems*.

Lynn, Johnny - (Jonathan Lynn; b. 1943) An English stage and film director, writer, producer and actor. Lynn directed Connie Booth in a stage production of *The Glass Menagerie* (1977). He also worked on *Twice a Fortnight* (1967), *Clue* (1985) and *Nuns on the Run* (1990).

Monaco – The Principality of Monaco is a sovereign city-state on the French Riviera.

Palin, Michael - (Sir Michael Edward Palin; b. 1943) Sir Michael was a member of Monty Python and went on to make several prominent travel documentaries. He also worked with John Cleese on *A Fish Called Wanda* (1988) and *Fierce Creatures* (1997).

Sanderson, Joan - (1912 – 1992) She was a British actress who had parts on *Ripping Yarns* (1979) and *The Great Muppet Caper* (1981). She played Mrs. Alice Richards in this episode.

Scott-Irvine, Garry – The managing director of John Cleese Production Thing (1998 –2012). He was John Cleese's personal assistant on *The Pink Panther 2* (2009) and *John Cleese: The Alimony Tour* (2011).

Scottish meanness joke – This is meanness in the English sense. It is a general lack of willingness to spend money taken to an extreme degree. Jokes about the Scots being mean were popular in England in the 1920s and 1930s.

Shannon, Johnny - (b. 1932) An English actor who appeared in *The Great Rock 'n' Roll Swindle* (1980) and *Stoned* (2005). He played Mr. Firkins in this episode.

Sotto voce – According to Oxford Languages, "sotto voce" means "(of singing or a spoken remark) sung or said in a quiet voice, as if not to be overheard."

Spiers, Bob - (Robert Alexander Spiers; 1945 – 2008) He was a Scottish television director and producer. Besides *Fawlty Towers* he worked on *Absolutely Fabulous* and *Spice World* (1997).

Whitehall farces - A series of farces that were produced for the Whitehall Theatre in London's West End. The theatre is currently called Trafalgar Theatre.

Baden Powell - (1796 – 1860) A priest in the Church of England and a mathematician at Oxford University. He held the Savilian Chair of Geometry from 1827 to 1860. There are multiple people with this name who could possibly fit in this context. The author has chosen who he feels is the most likely match.

Benzedrine – A type of amphetamine.

Birmingham – A metropolitan borough in the West Midlands, it is the second-largest city in the United Kingdom.

Bit of crumpet – British slang for "a very sexually desirable woman."

Brilliantine – A kind of scented oil used by men to make their hair look glossy. It was created around the start of the twentieth century by French perfumer Éd. Pinaud, a company founded by Édouard Pinaud (1810 – 1868).

Cognac – A type of brandy named after the commune in Cognac, France.

Colchester – A city in Essex, East of England. It occupies the site of Camulodunum, the capital of Roman Britain.

English Riviera – A coastal location in the county of Devon. It consists of Torquay, Paignton, Brixham and the smaller village of Babbacombe. The English Riviera is also referred to as Torbay.

Faith healer – Someone who uses religious belief and prayer in place of medical treatment.

Freud, Sigmund - (Sigismund Schlomo Freud; 1856 – 1939) An Austrian neurologist who founded psychoanalysis.

Game pie – According to Oxford Languages, "game pie" is "a pie made with meat from wild mammals or birds."

Gladstone – (William Ewart Gladstone; 1809 – 1898) A British Liberal politician whose highest office was Prime Minister, a post he held for twelve years.

Golden Dog, The – Ancient Egyptian restaurant that Basil suggests instead of the French restaurant.

Haig, Earl – A peerage of the United Kingdom. Sybil is probably referring to the first Earl Haig, Field Marshall Sir Douglas Haig (1861 – 1928). He commanded the British Expeditionary Force on the Western Front during World War I from 1915 until the end of the war.

Hayseed – A simple person from the countryside.

Johnson, Lyndon - (Lyndon Baines Johnson; 1908 – 1973) Johnson was the 36th President of the United States of America. He has been lauded for domestic issues like health care, welfare, education and civil rights. Conversely, he has been criticized for foreign policies, especially the Vietnam War.

Johnson, Mrs., the late president's wife - (Claudia Alta "Lady Bird" Johnson, née Taylor; 1912 – 2007) She was married to Lyndon Johnson and was the First Lady of the United States (1963 – 1969).

Leek House – The name of a, probably fictional, Welsh restaurant in Torquay. The name was probably chosen because the national emblem of Wales is the leek.

Load of cobblers – A cockney rhyming slang. The term "cobblers' awls" means "balls" or testicles.

Mad as March hares - An English idiom referring to the antics of the European hare (*Lepus europaeus*) during its mating season, March.

Male menopause – A term that some use to describe the decrease in testosterone that comes with aging.

Mediterranean type – Someone with the physical characteristics of people found in southern Europe.

Melody Maker - A British weekly music magazine founded by composer Lawrence Wright (Frederick Lawrence Wright; 1888 – 1964) in 1926.

Newcastle – Newcastle upon Tyne is a city in Tyne and Wear, England.

Orchard Street – There is an Orchard Road in Torbay, Torquay. It is possible that the name Orchard Street was used or even invented by Cleese and Booth because, in this episode, there is a French restaurant there whose name translates as "The Apple of Love."

Piltdown ponce – A primitive, unmanly human being.

Port – A kind of fortified wine from the Douro Valley in northern Portugal.

Private parts – A way of referring to the genitals.

Puff adder – A highly venomous viper that inhabits grasslands and savannahs. It is also known as the African puff adder or the common puff adder.

Saint Christopher – The patron saint of travelers, he was a martyr killed in the third century during the reign of emperor Maximinus Daia (270 – 313 CE).

Speaking Clock – A live or recorded voice service that one could call to hear the time of day.

Stick Insect – An order of insects known as Phasmatodea that appear thin and often long.

"To sleep perchance to dream" - A quote from *Hamlet* by William Shakespeare (1564 – 1616) where Prince Hamlet is contemplating suicide. The sleep here means "death."

Tommyrot – An informal, dated expression meaning "nonsense" or "rubbish."

Torquay - A seaside town in Devon, England.

French:

> **La Pomme d'Amour** - The Apple of Love (the French restaurant that is on Orchard Street).

> **Moi** - Me

Mon plaisir – My pleasure

Italian:

> **Outro** - A passage that concludes a piece of music.
>
> **Stupidissimo** - Stupid

Spanish:

> **Un altero. Pronto! Pronto! Pronto! -** Another one. Quickly! Quickly! Quickly!
>
> **Socorro! Socorro! -** Help! Help!
>
> **Si Si** – Yes, yes.

From the commentary by John Cleese

Barker, Ronnie - (Ronald William George Barker; 1929 – 2005) An English actor, writer and comedian who had his big television break on *The Frost Report* (1966 – 1967). It was there that he first worked with John Cleese.

Baroness – The female equivalent of a baron. It can also mean the wife or widow of a baron.

Bedford – A market town in Bedfordshire, England.

Bickford-Smith, Imogen - (b. 1952) An English actress who was in *Monty Python's The Meaning of Life* (1983) and *A Fish Called Wanda* (1988). She played the part of the girlfriend in this episode.

68

Bragg, Melvyn - (Melvyn Bragg, Baron Bragg; b. 1939) An English broadcaster, author and parliamentarian. Best known for *The South Bank Show* (1978 – 2010, 2012 -) and *In Our Time* (1998 -).

Clifton College – A public school in Bristol, South West England.

Colchester - A city in Essex, East of England. It occupies the site of Camulodunum, the capital of Roman Britain.

Cook, David – According to John Cleese, this is someone associated with *The Frost Report* (1966 – 1967).

Corbett, Ronnie - (Ronald Balfour Corbett; 1930 – 2016) A Scottish actor, writer and comedian who had his big television break on *The Frost Report* in 1966. It was there that he first worked with John Cleese.

Frost Report, The - (1966-67) A satirical show that was hosted by Sir David Frost (David Paradine Frost; 1939 – 2013) that introduced John Cleese to television.

Gladstone - (William Ewart Gladstone; 1809 – 1898) A British Liberal politician whose highest office was Prime Minister, a post he held for twelve years.

Gormless – According to Oxford Languages, it is an informal British term meaning "lacking sense or initiative; foolish."

Gray, Elspet - (Elspet Jean Gray, Baroness Rix; 1929 – 2013) A Scottish actress who was in *Black Adder* (1983) and *Four Weddings and a Funeral* (1994). She played the part of Dr. Abbott in this episode.

Henson, Basil - (1918 – 1990) An English actor who was in *The Frozen Dead* (1966) and *Arthur? Arthur!* (1969). He played the part of Dr. Abbott in this episode.

Henson, Nicky - (Nicholas Victor Leslie Henson; 1945 – 2019) He first met John Cleese while working on *The Frost Report* (1966). He also played a part in *Downton Abbey* (2010 – 2013) and was a regular member of the cast of *EastEnders* beginning in 2006. He played Mr. Johnson in this episode.

Lord – A member of the peerage.

MacMillan, Harold - (Maurice Harold Macmillan, 1st Earl of Stockton; 1894 – 1986) A conservative politician who served as Prime Minister of the United Kingdom from 1957 to 1963. He opposed the appeasement of Germany and supported the welfare state and mixed economy.

Mencap – The Royal Mencap Society, a UK-based charity that helps people with learning disabilities.

Miles, Rayleen – The wife of Tony Miles who was a friend of John Cleese' and who worked in an Australian ad agency.

Peters, Luan - (b. Carol Ann Hirsch, aka Karol Keyes; 1946 – 2017) An English actress who appeared in several Hammer films. She played Rayleen Miles in this episode.

Rix, Brian - (Brian Norman Roger Rix, Baron Rix; 1924 – 2016) Rix was an English stage actor, manager and producer. He had tremendous success producing farces for the London stage.

Skynner, Robin - (1922 – 2000) A pioneer in the field of mental health, he worked with John Cleese. Together they wrote the books *Families and How to Survive Them* (1983) and *Life and How to Survive It* (1993).

Stevenage – A large town and borough in Hertfordshire, England.

Sybil's mother – Sybil's mother's personality was based on that of John Cleese's mother.

Weston-super-Mare - A seaside town in Somerset, England. It is where John Cleese lived during much of his childhood.

Winner, Michael – A film director perhaps best known for movies like *Death Wish* (1974). He worked with John Cleese on *Bullseye!* (1990) and *Parting Shots* (1998).

Episode Nine – Waldorf Salad

Bidford Bridge – A bridge dating from the early 15th century that crosses the Avon at Bidford-on-Avon, Warwickshire, England.

Bit of crumpet - British slang for "a very sexually desirable woman."

British Tourist Board - The government agency set up to provide tourist information to visitors.

Butterball - Usually, the term "butterball" is used to refer to someone who is overweight. However, in this case it may be used to mean a "sucker."

"Can't get a drink after 3:00, can't eat after 9:00. Is the war still on?" - Mr. Hamilton is referring first to the law that pubs had to stop selling alcohol in Great Britain after 3:00pm and could not resume until later. In the second instance, he is referring to the fact that Basil Fawlty has just informed him that the cooking staff leaves at 9:00pm. Hamilton asks about the war still being on because during World War II there was strict rationing in effect.

Chin wag – A friendly chat.

Cold meat salad – A type of salad that can consist of cold cuts (sandwich meats) by themselves or with a variety of vegetables or other salad ingredients.

Cornwall – A historic county and ceremonial county in South West England. It is the homeland of the Cornish people and is one of the Celtic nations.

72

Crummy dump – According to Oxford Languages, "crummy" means "dirty, unpleasant, or of poor quality." Also according to Oxford languages, "dump" means "an unpleasant or dreary place."

Donald Duck - (Donald Fauntleroy Duck; b. 1934) A creation of The Walt Disney Company. Donald's first appearance was in *The Little Wise Hen* (1934).

Dorchester – There is a small amount of confusion between Sybil and Mr. Hamilton. Sybil says that Terry used to work "at Dorchester." Mr. Hamilton thinks that Sybil means the famous London hotel, but she clarifies and says that Terry worked in Dorchester. The Dorchester is a swanky hotel that has had many famous guests. Dorchester is a historic market town and county town of Dorset, England.

Eastbourne - A seaside resort town in East Sussex, England.

Fob off – There are three definitions from the Merriam-Webster Dictionary that could apply to the circumstances of this episode. "1. to put off with a trick, excuse, or inferior substitute. 2. to pass or offer (something spurious) as genuine. 3. to put aside."

Forster, E. M. - (Edward Morgan Forster; 1879 – 1970) Forster was an English writer known for *A Room With a View* (1908), *Howards End* (1910) and more.

Free market – According to Oxford Languages, "free market" means "an economic system in which prices are determined by unrestricted competition between privately owned businesses."

Green Stamps – S & H Green Stamps were a popular form of trading stamp in the U. S. The program was started in 1896 by Thomas Sperry (Thomas Alexander Sperry; 1864 – 1913) and Shelley Byron Hutchinson (1864 – 1961). When consumers made purchases at retailers, they were given green stamps. These stamps could be traded in for items from a catalog.

Karate – Also known as karate-do, it is a Japanese and Okinawan martial art first developed in the Ryukyu Kingdom.

M5 Motorway – A motorway in England that links the Midlands with the South West.

Mickey Mouse money – A rude utterance sometimes used by Americans traveling abroad. The implication is that the foreign money is colorful and valueless. Mickey Mouse (created 1928) is a cartoon mouse who was co-created in 1928 by Walt Disney (Walter Elias Disney; 1901 – 1966) and Ub Iwerks (Ubbe Ert Iwerks; 1901 – 1971). Mickey Mouse is the mascot of The Walt Disney Company.

Never Love a Stranger - (1948) The debut novel by Harold Robbins (1916 – 1997). In 1958 it became a film starring John Drew Barrymore (b. John Blythe Barrymore, Jr.; 1932 – 2004), Robert Bray (Robert E. Bray; 1917 – 1983) and Steve McQueen (Terrence Stephen McQueen; 1930 – 1980).

Plaice - A type of North Atlantic flatfish.

Poodle – A breed of water dog that was originally bred for hunting. They are known for their fur which continues to grow rather than being shed.

Pornographic Muzak – Basil refers to the novels of Harold Robbins (1916 – 1997) as "pornographic Muzak." Pornographic in the sense that they appeal to a reader's libido more so than provide aesthetic value. Also, Muzak because the novels are not stimulating in any intellectual way. Muzak is a brand of American music intended to stay in the background and not intrude too much into consciousness.

Proust, Marcel – (Valentin Louis Georges Eugène Marcel Proust; 1871 – 1922) Proust was a French novelist known for *Remembrance of Things Past.*

Right-O – An informal way of saying "yes," most commonly used in Australia and Canada.

Ritz salad – According to Basil, a Ritz salad is apples, grapefruit and potatoes in a mayonnaise sauce. The Ritz London is a top-rated hotel in Piccadilly, London, England. First opened in 1906 by César Ritz (b. Cäsar Ritz; 1850 – 1918), the hotel has long been associated with luxury and elegance.

Robbins, Harold - (1916 – 1997) An American writer who penned popular novels. He had 25 bestsellers and sold more than 750 million books. *Never Love a Stranger* was his debut novel in 1948.

Salt cellar – According to Oxford Languages, a salt cellar is "a dish or container for storing salt, now typically a closed container with perforations in the lid for sprinkling." In the United States, the equivalent is a saltshaker.

Socialism – A very basic definition from Oxford Languages: Socialism is a "political and economic theory of social organization which advocates that the means of production, distribution, and exchange should be owned or regulated by the community as a whole."

Tete-a-tete – A private conversation between two people.

Tripe – An informal way of saying "rubbish."

Waldorf salad – A salad that was created at the Waldorf-Astoria Hotel in New York City. It was originally created for a ball in honor of the St. Mary's Hospital for Children which took place March 13, 1896. There are many variations presented on the internet, but it is generally made from celery, apples, walnuts and grapes in mayonnaise. It is served on a bed of lettuce. Contrary to the beliefs of some people, there is no cheese in the recipe.

Western Europe – During the Cold War, Western Europe was used to describe the parts of the continent that were not in the East Bloc.

Wrong side of the road – In the United Kingdom, cars are driven on the left side of the road. This contrasts to Mr. Hamilton's home country of the United States where cars are driven on the right.

French:

Bon appetit – Enjoy your meal.

German:

Raus - (Get) Out

Spanish:

Adios – Good bye

From the commentary by John Cleese

Art of Complaining, The – One of the many soft skill videos produced by Video Arts. *see also Video Arts below*

Ass -

> **Bust his ass** - To upbraid someone until he does something.
>
> **Get your ass over here** - Come to me right now.
>
> **He's a horse's ass** - He is a stupid and foolish person.
>
> **Move his ass** - Hurry him up.
>
> **Put his ass in a sling** – Severely punish a person.

Back acting – When the actors have their backs turned to the audience.

Bird, Norman - (John George Norman Bird; 1924 – 2005) An English actor who worked alongside Lawrence Olivier (Laurence Kerr Olivier, Baron Olivier; (1907 – 1989) in *Term of Trial* (1962) and Sir Sean Connery (Thomas Connery; 1930 – 2020) in *The Hill* (1965). In this episode he played Mr. Arrad.

Boa, Bruce - (Andrew Bruce Boa; 1930 – 2004) A Canadian actor who had parts in *The Empire Strikes Back* (1980) and *Full Metal Jacket* (1987). He played Mr. Hamilton in this episode.

Conoley, Terence - (1919 – 2016) An English actor who had roles in *A Fish Called Wanda* (1988) and *The Fall and Rise of Reginald Perrin* (1976 – 1977). In *A Touch of Class* he played Mr. Wareing. In *Waldorf Salad* he played Mr. Johnston.

Dawes, Anthony - (Anthony Cecil John Dawes; 1928 – 2021) He was an English character actor who had roles in *The Avengers* (1967) and *Barry Lyndon* (1975). In this episode he played Mr. Libson.

Ellis, June - (June Georgina Ellis Bromley; 1926 – 2011) An English actress who had roles in *The Prisoner* (1967) and *All Creatures Great and Small* (1978 – 1989). She played Mrs. Johnston in this episode.

Fierce Creatures - (1997) A comedy film written by John Cleese and Iain Johnstone (1943 – 2023) and directed by Robert Young (Robert William Young; b. 1933) and Fred Schepisi (Frederic Alan Schepisi; b. 1939). It stars John Cleese, Michael Palin (b. 1943), Jamie Lee Curtis (b. 1958) and Kevin Kline (b. 1947). The film is about financial difficulties and the ensuing shenanigans at a zoo.

Fish Called Wanda, A - (1988) A comedy film written by John Cleese and Charles Crichton (Charles Ainslie Crichton; 1910 – 1999) and starring John Cleese, Michael Palin (Sir Michael Edward Palin; b. 1943), Jamie Lee Curtis (b. 1958) and Kevin Kline (Kevin

Delaney Kline; b. 1947). It is a heist film featuring a barrister, femme fatale, and incompetent crooks.

Jay, Tony - (1933 – 2006) An actor who was a former member of the Royal Shakespeare Company. He moved into film and voice acting. He was in Terry Gilliam's (b. 1940) movie *Time Bandits* (1981) along with John Cleese.

Johnstone, Iain – (1943 – 2023) An English writer, broadcaster and television producer. He co-wrote *Fierce Creatures* (1997) and made several documentaries including one about *Monty Python's The Meaning of Life* (1983) and one about *A Fish Called Wanda* (1988).

Nielson, Claire - (née Isbister; b. 1937) A Scottish actress who appeared in *The Two Ronnies* (1971 – 1983) and *Scotch & Wry* (1978 – 1980). In this episode she played Mrs. Hamilton.

Robinson, Peter - One of the founders of Video Arts.

Santa Barbara – A coastal city in Santa Barbara County, California.

Tanner, Stella - (1925 – 2012) An English actress who had roles in *Murder Most Foul* (1964) and *Dixon of Dock Green* (1964 – 1974). In this episode she was Mrs. Arrad.

Video Arts - A UK video training company for professionals. It was founded in 1972 by John Cleese (b. 1939) and Sir Antony Jay (Antony Rupert Jay; 1930 – 1916). The idea behind the company was to make entertaining videos to help people better learn the skills presented therein.

Bangers á la bang - "Bangers" is an informal British word for sausages. "A la" is French for "in the style of." Polly is saying sausages in the style of a "bang." It's her way of saying that by adding hot sauce to the sausages, they will make a bang when the dog eats them. She is comparing the surprise that the dog will get to the suddenness and intensity of an explosion.

Barcelona - The largest city and capital of Catalonia which is an autonomous region of Spain.

Book of Remembrance – A book memorializing people who have died.

British Leyland – British Leyland Motor Corporation Ltd (BLMC) was a car manufacturing conglomerate formed in 1968. It was the merger of Leyland Motors and British Motor Holdings. It was partly nationalized in 1975 when the UK government made a holding company named British Leland.

Burma Railway – Also known as the Death Railway it extends from Ban Pong, Thailand to Thanbyuzayat, Burma (now called Myanmar). It was constructed during the Second World War. About 90,000 civilians and 12,000 allied troops died during the construction.

Butlin's - A chain of seaside resorts located primarily in the UK. They were designed to provide affordable holiday options for British families.

Calcutta – Also known as Kolkata, it is the capital of West Bengal, India.

Cheese footballs – A British version of cheese balls. The balls are made to look like little footballs (soccer balls).

Continental Breakfast - A lighter breakfast, generally consisting of breads and a hot beverage.

Full Breakfast - A heartier breakfast that includes cooked items such as eggs, bacon and sausages.

Gettysburg Address – One of the most famous speeches in U. S. history, it was delivered by President Abraham Lincoln (1809 – 1865) on November 19, 1863. The speech was delivered four and a half months after the Battle of Gettysburg. The speech is known for its conciseness, among other aspects.

Jumper – The British term for what Americans call a "sweater."

Kipper – A herring that has been preserved with salt and then smoke.

Leeman, Mr. - Named after Andrew Leeman, a restaurateur at the Savoy. His stories of having to remove deceased guests gave Cleese the idea for this episode.

M. D. – Managing Director

Modern dress – A type of attire that is more up to date than what is normally expected from someone in their line of work. For example, perhaps undertakers would be expected to wear top hats and a tuxedo with tails. The term probably comes from theater and film. According to Oxford Languages, "modern dress" means "costumes for a theatrical production that are in a style from the period of performance rather than that of a play's setting or time of writing."

Oh, What a Beautiful Mornin' - This is the opening song from the Broadway musical *Oklahoma!* (1943) by Richard Rodgers (Richard Charles Rodgers; 1902 – 1979) and Oscar Hammerstein II (Oscar Greeley Clendenning Hammerstein II; 1895 – 1960).

Ronay, Egon - (Egon Miklos Ronay; 1915 – 2010) A Hungarian-born restaurant and hotel critic who wrote guides to Irish and British restaurants.

Shih Tzu – A dog breed from Tibet. It was probably bred from Pekinese and Lhasa Apso. They are not known for stalking reindeer.

Socialism - A very basic definition from Oxford Languages: Socialism is "a political and economic theory of social organization which advocates that the means of production, distribution, and exchange should be owned or regulated by the community as a whole."

Telegraph, The – A visual reference. It may just be the newspaper that the prop people had on hand. It's a broadsheet newspaper founded in 1855.

Ticket – The Major looks at Mr. Leeman and says, "He doesn't look quite the ticket." In this case "ticket" means a strong or healthy person. Therefore, the Major is saying that Mr. Leeman looks weak.

Violin concerto – A piece of music written to be performed by a solo violin. The violin is accompanied by a full orchestra or other instrumental ensemble.

Watney's Red Barrel - Another visual reference. It is likely just what the prop department chose to place in the set. Watney's Red Barrel is a bitter sold in the United Kingdom and especially popular during the 1960s and 1970s. Brewed by Watney, Combe and Reid in London.

French:

> **Tout de suite** – Right now

Spanish:

> **Por favor, el perro microscopico** – Please, the microscopic dog.

> **¿Cómo?** - How?

> **Más grande** – Bigger

> **¿Qué?** - What?

From the commentary by John Cleese

Argent, Douglas - (Douglas George Charles Argent; 1921 – 2010) Argent was the producer of *Fawlty Towers* during the second series. He also produced episodes for *The Prince of Denmark* (1974) and *Steptoe and Son* (1974).

Benson, Elizabeth - (b. 1926) Benson played Mrs. Heath in *Gourmet Night* and Mrs. White in *The Kipper and the Corpse*. She was also in *Dr. Finlay's Casebook* (1967) and *The Agatha Christie Hour* (1982).

Buchner, Pamela - (b. 1939) Buchner played Miss Young in this episode. She was also in *Dixon of Dock Green* (1967 – 1968) and *The Gentle Touch* (1980 – 1983).

Davies, Richard - (Dennis Wilfred Davies; 1926 – 2015) Davies was a Welsh actor who played Mr. White in this episode. He was also in *The Lavender Hill Mob* (1951) and *Coronation Street* (1974 – 1975).

Farceur – According to Oxford language, a farceur is "a writer or performer in farces."

Fish Called Wanda, A - (1988) A comedy film written by John Cleese and Charles Crichton (Charles Ainslie Crichton; 1910 – 1999) and starring John Cleese, Michael Palin (Sir Michael Edward Palin; b. 1943), Jamie Lee Curtis (b. 1958) and Kevin Kline (Kevin Delaney Kline; b. 1947). It is a heist film featuring a barrister, femme fatale, and incompetent crooks.

Gilliam, Terry - (Terence Vance Gilliam; b. 1940) Gilliam is an animator and film director. He is a member of Monty Python. He directed *Brazil* (1985) and *The Man Who Killed Don Quixote* (2018).

Hitchcock, Alfred - (Sir Alfred Joseph Hitchcock; 1899 – 1980) Hitchcock was an English filmmaker, who created a famous shower scene in the film *Psycho* (1960).

Ingrams, Richard - (Richard Reid Ingrams; b. 1937) The co-founder and second editor of the satirical *Private Eye* magazine.

McBain, Robert – (1932 – 2004) McBain played the part of Mr. Xerxes in this episode. He was also in *A Fish Called Wanda* (1988) and various Video Arts training videos.

McKeown, Charles - (b. 1946) McKeown worked with Monty Python playing small roles in *Monty Python's Life of Brian* (1979). He wrote the sitcom *Hold the Sunset* (2018) which starred Cleese. He played Mr. Ingrams in this episode.

Marten, Len - (1920 – 1990) Marten played a hotel guest in this episode. He also appeared in *The Crimson Tide Permanent Assurance* segment of *Monty Python's The Meaning of Life* (1983).

Mason, Raymond - (1924 – 2022) Mason played Mr. Zebedee in this episode. He was in many productions including *The New Avengers* (1976) and *The Les Dawson Show* (1978).

Palmer, Geoffrey - (Geoffrey Dyson Palmer; 1927 – 2020) Palmer played Dr. Price in this episode. He worked with John Cleese on several projects including *Fairly Secret Army* (1986), *The Pink Panther 2* (2009), *A Fish Called Wanda* (1988) and various training films for Video Arts.

Private Eye – Founded in 1961, *Private Eye* is a British satirical and current affairs magazine.

Pugh, Mavis - (Mavis Gladys Fox Pugh; 1914 – 2006) Pugh played the part of Mrs. Chase in this episode. She was also in *Are You Being Served?* (1976 – 1978) and *Dad's Army* (1974).

Royle, Derek - (1928 – 1990) He was an English actor. He had roles in the Beatles' *Magical Mystery Tour* (1967) and *The Benny Hill Show* (1985). Royle played Mr. Leeman in this episode of *Fawlty Towers*.

Spiers, Bob - (Robert Alexander Spiers; 1945 – 2008) He was a Scottish television director and producer. Besides *Fawlty Towers* he worked on *Absolutely Fabulous* (1992 – 2001) and *Spice World* (1997).

Terry-Thomas - (Thomas Terry Hoar Stevens; 1911 – 1990) An English character actor and comedian. Known for the gap in his front teeth and for playing notorious upper-class roles.

Video Arts - A UK video training company for professionals. It was founded in 1972 by John Cleese (b. 1939) and Sir Antony Jay (Antony Rupert Jay; 1930 – 1916). The idea behind the company was to make entertaining videos to help people better learn the skills presented therein.

Technical talk:

> **Three shot** – In movies and television, a three shot shows three subjects in the frame at one time.
>
> **Vision mixer** – According to the Oxford Languages, a vision mixer is "a person whose job is to select and manipulate images in television broadcasting or recording." In other words, the person who switches between cameras and adds visual effects during recording and/or broadcasting.

Barcelona - The largest city and capital of Catalonia which is an autonomous region of Spain.

Battle of Agincourt – An English victory during the Hundred Years' War between England and France. The battle occurred on October 25, 1415, also known as St. Crispin's Day. The French outnumbered the English during the battle and the English victory proved to be a real morale booster for the English.

Bit of gyp - A British term mean an uncomfortable amount of pain but nothing too serious.

Bogey – A bit of nasal mucous.

Cheerio – In British English, it is an informal way of saying "goodbye."

Chicken Andaluse – Terry's way of saying "Chicken Andalusia." Andalusian-style chicken is a dish that originated in Andalusia, an autonomous region of Spain. There are variations of the recipe to be found online and in cookbooks.

Choc ice – British term for "chocolate ice cream" often served as a frozen block.

Cockney - An English dialect and accent spoken primarily in the East End of London by the working-class and the lower middle-class.

Crécy - The Battle of Crécy (August 26, 1346) was a battle during the Hundred Years War. The French army was led by King Philip VI (1293 – 1350) and the English by King Edward III (1312 – 1377).

Crisps – The British term for "potato chips."

Cross to bear – A problem that causes worry or trouble for a person over a long period of time. It is a metaphor for the cross that Jesus carried in the *Bible*.

Do – An affair or party.

Eel pie – A dish made from cooked eels placed in a pie crust and baked. For a time, it was quite popular in London's East End.

Eggplant Español - An eggplant recipe from Spain or Mexico. There are many variations of the dish.

Fête - A celebration.

Franco Fritters – Probably a made-up dish that pokes fun at Franco's (Francisco Franco Bahamonde; 1892 – 1975) rule in Spain and his influence on culture there.

Gazpacho – A Spanish tomato soup served ice cold.

Gin and It – A cocktail also known as a sweet martini. The "it" refers to sweet vermouth. It is garnished with maraschino cherries.

Marx Brothers film – Films by the Marx Brothers, Groucho (Julius Henry Marx; 1890 – 1977), Chico (Leonard Joseph Marx; 1887 – 1961), Harpo (Arthur Marx, b. Adolph Marx; 1888 – 1964) and Zeppo (Herbert Manfred Marx; 1901 – 1979) were known for the madcap antics of the brothers.

Medium sherry – A half-sweet sherry composed around a lighter style like Amontillado.

Natter – Casual talk about unimportant things.

Nervous breakdown – According to the Mayo Clinic, a nervous breakdown is described as the following: "Nervous breakdown isn't a medical term, nor does it indicate a specific mental illness. But that doesn't mean it's a normal or a healthy response to stress. What some people call a nervous breakdown may indicate an underlying mental health problem that needs attention, such as depression or anxiety."

Northern accent – An accent from a group of dialects in Northern English. It has been influenced by the Northumbrian dialect of Middle English, Old Norse brought by the Vikings and Irish English which added its influence after the Great Famine.

Ode to Joy – A poem (1785) by Friedrich Schiller (Johann Christoph Friedrich von Schiller; 1759 – 1805) that was later changed somewhat by Ludwig van Beethoven (bapt. 1770 – 1827) when he included it in his Ninth Symphony (1824).

Old man – In the UK this is often an affectionate term for a male friend.

Paella - The name "paella" comes from the Valencian word for frying pan. The principal ingredients are rice, chicken, rabbit, vegetables, green beans, lima beans and saffron.

Petrol – British for "gasoline."

Poitiers – Battle of Poitiers (September 19, 1356) was a battle during the Hundred Years War. The French were led by King John II (1319 – 1364) and the Anglo-Gascon force was led by Edward, The Black Prince (Edward of Woodstock; 1330 – 1376).

Semaphore – A system of communication that involves holding up flags to represent letters of the alphabet.

Steady on – A British way of saying "calm down."

Torquay - A seaside town in Devon, England.

Trafalgar – The Battle of Trafalgar (October 21, 1805) was a naval engagement. The British Royal Navy fought the French and Spanish Navies. It was during The War of the Third Coalition (1805) during the Napoleonic Wars (1803 – 1815).

Up yours! - A rude reply to someone. In this case, Roger disguises it as a toast for humorous effect.

Wilde, Oscar - (Oscar Fingal O'Flahertie Wills Wilde; 1854 – 1900) was an Irish writer. Best known for *The Importance of Being Earnest* (1895) and *The Picture of Dorian Gray* (1890).

Wog - A derogatory term used in British English to mean anyone who is not white.

Yom Kippur – The Day of Atonement, it is the holiest day in Judaism and Samaritanism.

Spanish:

Arriba – Come on

Vamos - Go

From the commentary by John Cleese

Alexander, Denyse - (Denyse Verena Macpherson; b. 1931) A British actress with roles in *Inspector Morse* (1987 – 2000) and *Heavy Weather* (1995). She played the part of Kitty in this episode of *Fawlty Towers*.

Ayckbourn, Alan - (b. 1939) A British playwright and director. He is known for plays like *Absurd Person Singular* (1975) and for putting unexpected emotions into farce. He also wrote a trilogy of plays called *The Norman Conquests* (1973).

Arnold, Robert – (1931 – 2003) A former British actor who appeared in productions like *Blake's Seven* (1979). Arnold plays the part of Arthur in this episode and the character is based on Cleese's Uncle Eric.

Campbell, Ken – (Kenneth Victor Campbell; 1941 – 2008) He played the part of Roger in this episode and was in *A Fish Called Wanda* (1988). In the commentary, Cleese mentions The Ken Campbell Road Show which was a theater group that performed in unconventional locations like pubs. Members of the group included Bob Hoskins (Robert William Hoskins; 1942 – 2014), Bernard Wrigley (b. 1948), Jane Wood, Dave Hill (David Hill; b. 1945) and Sylvester McCoy (Percy James Patrick Kent-Smith; b. 1943).

Clockwise - (1986) A British comedy film starring John Cleese, written by Michael Frayn (b. 1933) and directed

92

by Christopher Morahan (Christopher Thomas Morahan; 1929 – 2017). It is a comedy about a headmaster who is obsessed with punctuality. He finds himself in a dilemma where he must fight to not be late for a Headmasters' Conference.

Colchester - A city in Essex, East of England. It occupies the site of Camulodunum, the capital of Roman Britain.

Frayn, Michael - (b. 1933) An English playwright and novelist. He is perhaps best known for his farce *Noises Off* (1982).

Henson, Nicky - (Nicholas Victor Leslie Henson; 1945 – 2019) He first met John Cleese while working on *The Frost Report* (1966). He also played a part in *Downton Abbey* (2010 – 2013) and was a regular member of the cast of *EastEnders* beginning in 2006. He played Mr. Johnson in *The Psychiatrist*.

Holloway, Julian - (b. 1944) A British actor known for being part of the *Carry On* franchise.

Hume, Roger – (1940 – 1996) He played the part of Reg in this episode. He also played a locksmith in *A Fish Called Wanda* (1988).

Ken Campbell Road Show – *see Ken Campbell above.*

McLean, Iain – The Internet Movie Database credits McLean with crew work on two episodes of *Fawlty Towers*, *The Anniversary* and *Basil the Rat*. John Cleese, in the commentary, credits him with the anagrams on the hotel sign.

Midget - The term "midget" is considered derogatory because of its roots in freak shows from the 1800's. The first known usage of the word was in 1816.

Norman Conquests, The *– see Alan Ayckbourn above*

Shaw, Christine - (1932 – 2003) She played the part of Sybil's friend, Audrey. Shaw also had roles in *The Avengers* (1963) and *Revenge of the Pink Panther* (1978).

"Stress makes you stupid." - *see Daniel Goleman under* Communication Problems.

Stubbs, Una - (1937 – 2021) She played the part of Alice in this episode. She was also married to Nicky Henson (Nicholas Victor Leslie Henson; 1945 – 2019) who played Mr. Johnson in *The Psychiatrist* episode of *Fawlty Towers.* Another *Fawlty Towers* connection is that she once performed alongside Winnie Atwell (Una Winifred Atwell; 1910 or 1914 – 1983), who was mentioned by The Major in the episode *Communication Problems.* Her father was the advisor to Cleese and Booth about the technical aspects of construction for *The Builders.*

Video Arts - A UK video training company for professionals. It was founded in 1972 by John Cleese (b. 1939) and Sir Antony Jay (Antony Rupert Jay; 1930 – 1916). The idea behind the company was to make entertaining videos to help people better learn the skills presented therein.

Weston-super-Mare - A seaside town in Somerset, England. It is where John Cleese lived during much of his childhood.

"You'll never waitress in Torquay again." - From the famous Hollywood line "You'll never work in this town again."

Technical talk:

> **Blocking** – The physical arrangement of actors on a film set.

Annie Hall - (1977) An award-winning American film by Heywood "Woody" Allen (b. Allen Stewart Konigsberg; b. 1935).

Babbacombe – A beach in Torquay.

Barcelona - The largest city and capital of Catalonia which is an autonomous region of Spain.

Beaujolais - The name of a wine from the Province of Beaujolais in France. The history of the wine can be traced back to the Roman Empire. Most of the Beaujolais wines are made with Gamay grapes. The grape has thin skin and is low in tannins. The wine itself is generally light-bodied and contains a high acid content.

Béarnaise - A traditional sauce for steak made with egg yolks, clarified butter, white wine, tarragon and a shallot reduction. It was created by chance by chef Jean-Louis Françoise-Collinet in 1836.

Beefeater gin – This is a visual reference. It is probably just what the prop department chose to place there.

Bomb scare - According to Oxford Languages a bomb scare or a bomb threat is "an alert prompted by the suspicion that a bomb has been planted in a public place."

Boycott, Geoffrey - (Sir Geoffrey Boycott; b. 1940) A former test cricketer who played for Yorkshire and England.

Bubonic Plague – One of three types of plague caused by the bacterium Yersinia pestis. It was first detected during the Bronze Age and still exists. It is a deadly disease that can be found in humans and some species of animals.

Bunch of fives – A fist.

Century – In cricket, a century is when a batsman scores 100 or more runs in a single inning.

Cheddar – A very popular cheese that originated in Cheddar, Somerset, England.

Cow eyes – A wide-eyed expression. Although it is generally an expression that has romantic intentions behind it, in this context the purpose is to elicit sympathy.

Cream crackers – Flat, normally square biscuit made from fermented dough and generally having a savory flavor.

Dago – An offensive term for someone who speaks Spanish, Portuguese or Italian.

Dander - "Getting one's dander up" meaning to "lose one's temper."

Danish Blue Cheese – Also known as Danablu, it is a Danish cheese made with Penicillium roqueforti. It is this mold that gives the cheese its blue qualities.

Digestive – A food or medicine that helps one's digestion.

Edam - A semi-hard cheese that originated in Edam, North Holland, The Netherlands. It both ages and travels well and does not spoil. It is packaged with a red rind of paraffin wax.

Filigree Siberian hamster – First of all, Manuel has a malapropism in mistaking "pedigree" and "filigree." Pedigree is used to describe the lineage of an animal or person. Filigree describes wire of gold or silver that is used for ornamental work. Secondly, it can be assumed that the pet shop owner said that the rat was from Siberia because it sounds exotic and is somewhat confusing. Finally, it is a rat and not a hamster.

Finger to nose – Basil taps his finger to the side of his nose to indicate that he understands.

Franco, Francisco - (General Francisco Franco Bahamonde; 1892 – 1975) Franco was the dictator of Spain from 1939 to 1975.

George Orwell's experience at Maxim's in Paris – *see George Orwell below*

Grotty - Unpleasant.

Hauté cuisine - According to Oxford languages, "hauté cuisine" is "the preparation and cooking of high-quality food following the style of traditional French cuisine."

Health and Safety Act - The Health and Safety at Work etc. Act 1974 (HSWA 1974, HASWA or HASAWA). It is an act of the UK Parliament that provides structure and authority for regulating workplace health and safety.

Her Majesty's Civil Servants – Employees of Her Majesty's Civil Service. They work in aspects of public life including education, defense, transportation and environment. Civil servants are employees of the Crown and not of Parliament.

Homing rat – Basil is comparing Manuel's rat to a homing pigeon. Homing pigeons are domestic birds that can find their way home even over long distances.

"How's the cat? It's gone to London to see the Queen!" - This comes from the English nursery rhyme *Pussy Cat, Pussy Cat* first published in 1805. The following is a popular version:

> Pussy cat, pussy cat, where have you been?
> I've been to London to visit/look at the Queen.
> Pussy cat, pussy cat, what did you do there?
> I frightened a little mouse under her/the chair.

Kamikaze – The kamikazes were Japanese pilots during World War II. They flew airplanes loaded with explosives and crashed them into their targets.

Mastermind – A British quiz show for the BBC that began in 1972. Bill Wright (1912 – 1980), the show's creator, got his inspiration from his experiences of being interrogated by the Gestapo during World War II.

Mooning about – A British idiom meaning to move about slowly due to unhappiness.

Old snoopy drawers – A childlike way of referring to someone who is making an investigation.

99

Orwell, George - (Eric Arthur Blair; 1903 – 1950) An English writer best known for his novels *Animal Farm* (1945) and *1984* (1949). Terry's remark about Orwell's experiences at Maxim's in Paris is a reference to his book *Down and Out in Paris and London* (1933).

Penzance - A port town in the Penwith district of Cornwall, England.

Piece of cake – Easy to do.

Pigeon/pidgin - A clever pun. A pigeon is, of course, a common type of bird. Pidgin English is a simplified version of English spoken by various groups around the world. It allows people who do not otherwise have a common language to communicate with each other more easily.

Plenty more fish in the sea – This is a phrase that is generally used to console someone whose romantic relationship has just ended.

Put to sleep - Euthanize

Ratatouille - A French Provençal dish made of stewed vegetables.

Ryvita – A rye-based crispbread originally manufactured by the Ryvita Company. The company was founded by John Edwin Garratt in Birmingham, England in 1925.

"Say goodnight to the folks, Gracie." - This was George Burns' last line whenever he performed with his wife, Gracie Allen.

Shipshape and Bristol fashion – This refers to a ship being in good and seamanlike condition.

Typical Latin - When Sybil refers to Manuel as a "typical Latin" she probably means because he is passionate and excitable. Those are stereotypes of Latin people.

Veal scallop – A thin piece of veal that has been hammered flat.

Vivaldi - (Antonio Lucio Vivaldi; 1678 – 1741) Vivaldi was an Italian composer. As Polly and Manuel are taking the rat to its new home, Vivaldi's Concierto de Aranjuez is playing on the soundtrack.

Watney's Red Barrel – Another visual reference. It is likely just what the prop department chose to place in the set. Watney's Red Barrel is a bitter sold in the United Kingdom and especially popular during the 1960s and 1970s. Brewed by Watney Combe and Reid in London.

Windsor soup – A British soup most often associated with the Victorian (1837 – 1901) and Edwardian (1901 –1910) eras. In the 1920s it became known as Brown Windsor soup. At that point it went from being an elegant soup made by famous chefs to becoming more of a gruel.

Wittgenstein, Ludwig - (Ludwig Josef Johann Wittgenstein; 1889 – 1951) He was an Austrian philosopher whose primary areas were logic, the philosophy of mathematics, the philosophy of mind and the philosophy of language.

French:

    Bon appétit - Enjoy your meal.

Spanish:

    Si - Yes

    Finito – Finished

    ¿Cómo? - How?

    Gracias – Thank you

    ¿Qué? - What?

    Esta aqui – It's here.

    ¿Qué ha pasado? - What happened?

    Un momentito – A little moment.

From the commentary by John Cleese

Carnegie, Mr. - Named after the hygiene inspector in the Royal Borough of Kensington who helped with the details when the script was being written.

Church, Suzanne - (b. 1951) Church is a British actress who had a role in *Fairly Secret Army* (1984) that was produced by Video Arts. The script for the first season of *Fairly Secret Army* was also edited by John Cleese. Church auditioned for the part of the Australian woman in the *The Psychiatrist*. In *Basil the Rat* she plays an uncredited hotel guest.

Cockney neighborhood – A working class neighborhood in London's East End.

Farce - According to Oxford Languages, a "farce" is "a comic dramatic work using buffoonery and horseplay and typically including crude characterization and ludicrously improbable situations." Cleese has described *Fawlty Towers* as a French farce, where a small lie is told to cover up a situation and then more and more lies must be told to make the first lie plausible.

Franklyn, Sabina - (Elizabeth Sabina Franklyn; b. 1954) A British actress who has played roles in the sitcoms *Keep It in the Family* (1980 – 1983) and *Full House* (1985 – 1986). In this episode of *Fawlty Towers* she played the part of Quentina.

Lang, Melody - (d. 2017) A former actress, writer and fashion designer who was married to Andrew Sachs. She played Mrs. Taylor in this episode of *Fawlty Towers*.

Neville, David – He is a former actor who became a psychotherapist. He was in the Michael Palin (Sir Michael Edward Palin; b. 1943)/Terry Jones (Terence Graham Parry Jones; 1942 – 2020) movie *Consuming Passions* (1988). He played Ronald in this episode of *Fawlty Towers*.

Taylor, James – A former British actor who was in *Star Wars: The Phantom Menace* (1999). In this episode he played Mr. Taylor.

Upper class – The highest social class in modern societies. It generally is comprised of the people with the most wealth and political power.

Sherwin, Stuart - (1927 – 2015) A former British actor who had roles in *Dad's Army* (1969 – 1972) and *Are You Being Served?* (1974 – 1976). He played a guest in this episode of *Fawlty Towers*.

Technical talk:

> **Mark -** An indicator showing an actor where to stand during a performance.

Made in the USA
Middletown, DE
22 October 2024

62725706R00060